The Four Roles of the
Numerate Learner

Effective teaching and assessment strategies to help
students think differently about mathematics

MARY FIORE

MARIA LUISA LEBAR

Pembroke Publishers Limited

© 2016 Pembroke Publishers
538 Hood Road
Markham, Ontario, Canada L3R 3K9
www.pembrokepublishers.com

Distributed in the U.S. by Stenhouse Publishers
480 Congress Street
Portland, ME 04101
www.stenhouse.com

Library and Archives Canada Cataloguing in Publication

Fiore, Mary, author
  The four roles of the numerate learner: effective teaching and assessment strategies to help students think differently about mathematics / Mary Fiore & Maria Luisa Lebar.

Issued in print and electronic formats.
ISBN 978-1-55138-311-8 (paperback).--ISBN 978-1-55138-915-8 (pdf)

1. Mathematics--Study and teaching (Elementary)--Evaluation.
2. Mathematics--Study and teaching (Early childhood)--Evaluation.
3. Effective teaching. I. Lebar, Maria Luisa, author II. Title.

QA135.6.F55 2016   372.7'044   C2016-900008-7
                                     C2016-900009-5

Editor: Janice Dyer
Cover Design: John Zehethofer
Typesetting: Jay Tee Graphics

Printed and bound in Canada
9 8 7 6 5 4 3

Acknowledgements

From Mary Fiore:

To Tata—my father—you have inspired me, from the heavens above, to be a *thinker*. The belief you had in me continues to guide me with strength and courage and I thank you for always expecting the best from me.

To Jonathan and *Alanna*—my children and my *fairytale*—you are precious in every way and the loves of my life. You have inspired me to believe, hope, and persevere, and I thank you from the depths of my soul.

To Maria Luisa—my friend and my co-author—you have made a dream a reality and I thank you for *thinking* and learning with me. Our lives will forever be intertwined!

From Maria Luisa Lebar:

To Andre—my soul mate, my pillar of strength—you always push my intellectual capacity to think differently. You are my force of inspiration to be a learner, innovator, creator, leader, and to just be me. Thank you for being my biggest fan and encouraging me to use my voice to influence and my words to ignite my purpose for sharing my narrative, motivated by my passion for literacy and teaching and learning.

To Angelica and *Austin*—my amazing children, the real *magic* and *love* in my life—your beautiful hearts and kind spirits inspire me to nurture my boundless possibilities and unleash my potential. Thank you for reminding me that my most important role in life is being your mother. You make it extraordinary and most gratifying!

To Nancy—my sister and kindred spirit—you are a remarkable educator with a compelling moral imperative to advocate for and ensure that every student has a voice. Your unwavering dedication and commitment to student learning and well-being are both inspirational and selfless. Thank you for motivating me to go for my dream!

To Mary—my friend and co-author—your passion for teaching and learning is contagious and so invigorating. Thank you for inviting me into your dream and learning with me to bring it to life. Our thinking has been a transformative experience!

This book is the product of our continuous questioning to support learning. Our commitment to student thinking and learning was the driving force behind the content of this book. Our independent learning journeys began many years ago, but our co-learning journey began just a few short years ago. We combined our passion and dedication for literacy and numeracy and the result was a new way of thinking for *the now*—a way of thinking that supports collaboration, creativity, innovation, reflection, and critical thinking.

Needless to say, our co-learning extends beyond us to include teachers, coordinators, administrators, consultants, coaches, superintendents, and students. We are most grateful to all of you. To Allan Luke, thank you for being our inspiration and for your continued support along this journey. To Marian Small, thank you for your support and for sharing your thinking, but most importantly, for your friendship. To Mary Macchiusi, thank you for believing in our purpose and presenting us with an opportunity to share our thinking with a broader audience. Finally, to Janice Dyer, thank you for your ongoing role as critical interpreter of our thoughts. Your support and suggestions have helped us to consolidate our thinking along this incredible journey.

Contents

Foreword

Education is a multi-faceted endeavour, and all educators benefit from considering many different perspectives on instruction and learning. Mary Fiore and Maria Luisa Lebar provide a unique approach to thinking about the critical elements of numeracy instruction. The focus of their work relates what we know about developing literate students to the development of numerate students.

I believe that teachers always benefit when connections are made between literacy and numeracy. This is true for teachers in the elementary panel who often adopt different teaching styles when teaching mathematics than when teaching literacy. It is also true for secondary teachers where, historically, the teaching of mathematics has been nothing like the teaching of humanities. The authors have created the *Four Roles of the Numerate Learner* framework based on work in literacy by Luke and Freebody that was subsequently adapted by the Ontario Ministry of Education and their own school board.

Reading about the four interconnected, but distinctive, categories will help the reader focus on different aspects of mathematics instruction that require attention in order to develop a numerate student who is able to successfully think through mathematical situations. Having a chapter focused on each role certainly clarifies what those roles actually look like. The authors' hope is that administrators and other educational leaders will acquaint their teachers and students with the framework so that all of them can be consciously aware of what goes into dealing with mathematical situations.

The authors draw on a wide variety of experts to support the development of the framework, and who support their beliefs about mathematics instruction. The authors help teachers identify appropriate learning conditions to foster critical literacy and numeracy. They clearly define what they mean by critical numeracy. They specifically address teaching strategies in all parts of a lesson, and discuss the role of assessment in the enterprise of creating numerate learners. The nature of this framework will help non-math teachers foster numeracy when they are engaged in teaching other subjects. The authors have included many examples of mathematics tasks, important questions to ask, and valuable assessment strategies for the classroom, both elementary and secondary.

Throughout the book are many questions for reflection that will support learning communities discussing the framework or other ideas expressed in the text. This resource successfully pulls together the work of experts, but refracted through a new and unique lens.

Marian Small

Mary Fiore's and Maria Luisa Lebar's *Four Roles of the Numerate Learner* framework exemplifies several educational principles that we have come to hold dear.

First, the function of curriculum is to "give perspective." Curriculum, in our estimation, is best seen as a metaphor for the lives we want to live and the people we want to be. The word "curriculum" then suggests a big picture. Using Allan Luke and Peter Freebody's *Four Resources Model*, the authors map out what it means to be a numerate learner. As they state, this involves not only skill, but also the ability to apply that skill to everyday life, and to use mathematics to inform and inquire. It also involves "critical mathematics literacy," which includes an understanding of the ways in which mathematics works to position us in particular ways that we may or may not wish to support.

Second, curriculum needs to be "generative." In other words, what is learned today has to be useful tomorrow. Under the best educational circumstances, what is learned today should support learners in outgrowing themselves, doing new and more challenging things tomorrow. The absence of this criterion is what is wrong with our old ways of doing mathematics. For instance, what students learn best from doing worksheets is how to do more worksheets. This is evident when students are given a written mathematical problem to solve that requires students to use a skill that they have seemly mastered through doing worksheets. The problem is too often there is no transfer—or very little transfer—from learning through worksheets to engaging in written mathematical problem solving. The engagements in the *Four Roles of the Numerate Learner* framework ensure that mastery of one dimension leads to the wherewithal to tackle the next, harder, more challenging mathematical problem. Rather than just "do mathematics," students learn to "think mathematically."

Third, "there is something that simply takes one's breath away by encountering good teaching." Mary Fiore and Maria Luisa Lebar practise good teaching. Good teachers are able to frame the work they do from different perspectives. From learning about critical literacy and studying Luke and Freebody's *Four Resources Model*, the authors recognized its application to mathematics and how that field might be rethought and retaught. Working with teachers in redesigning curriculum, they and their colleagues have created a stunning array of mathematical engagements. In short, as teacher-leaders and curriculum researchers, they open our eyes and the eyes of readers to a new set of possibilities for how to approach problems in the teaching of mathematics, as well as how to overcome them.

This volume sets a new bar for all of us. It personifies some education principles that merit longevity and emulation. When this volume is used to its best advantage, it will become a generative catalyst that is bound to revitalize and revalue not only mathematics education, but also education more generally. Our compliments to the authors. May it be used conceptually to see the big picture, generatively to revitalize mathematics instruction, and demonstratively to encourage teachers everywhere to grow from a basis of current best practice. As the authors emphasize, the *Four Roles of the Numerate Learner* framework is a starting point, not a resting spot.

Jerome C. Harste and Vivian M. Vasquez

Preface

"I teach because I search, because I question, and because I submit myself to questioning."
Freire, 1998, p. 35

Teaching and learning in the twenty-first century—*the now*—are multi-faceted activities. We need students to become skilled critical thinkers, thoughtful problem solvers, and reflective communicators. To achieve this vision, educators strive to create a connected classroom culture that is built on trust and mutual respect, and where students are able to ask questions, pose problems, explore ideas, and make informed decisions. Building capacity for connectedness supports an environment that is empowering and engaging, where students are meaningfully involved, where relevance is key, and where their voice matters.

The essence of every teaching and learning experience for *the now* is to create a democratic learning environment with critical thinking at the forefront, where we build success for all students. To do this, we need to consider and question the status quo and question our current understanding of literacy and numeracy. As co-authors, we began by linking critical literacy to critical numeracy. We explored the fine differences among *literacy*, *new literacies*, and *critical literacy*, recognizing that they are conceptually integrated. Critical literacy builds on the fundamental principles of literacy by providing a lens for viewing the world from multiple perspectives and creating classroom cultures that value diversity, multi-literacies, and our students' cultural experiences. To help students adopt a critical stance, they are invited to question the authority of texts and identify and examine the author's bias or perspective, then engage in dialogue and discourse about text, relating it to their daily lives and their own point of view. At the same time, we examined the connections between *mathematical knowledge*, *numeracy*, and *critical numeracy*. We used our thinking about critical literacy to build our understanding of critical numeracy.

The goal of mathematics teaching for *the now* is to support the development of a numerate learner, with a focus on numeracy and its relationship to mathematics. Numeracy and mathematics share an inherent relationship. On the one hand, skills like critical thinking and problem solving, applying technology, and understanding ideas and information require a solid grounding in mathematical skills and concepts. On the other hand, knowledge of mathematical skills and concepts alone is not enough to guarantee numeracy (Ontario Ministry of Education, Literacy and Numeracy Secretariat, 2012). When numeracy is embedded in all curricular areas, it will deepen students' understanding of cross-curricular content and enhance their capacity to lead informed lives (Steen, 2001). Our vision of mathematics teaching for the twenty-first century extends beyond the numerate learner to include the *critically* numerate learner. A critically numerate learner recognizes that mathematics used in practical situations has the potential to be politically and morally loaded (Stroessiger, 2002). Critical numeracy, which builds on numeracy, entails questioning the source(s) of mathematical information in a variety of forms. It involves examining mathematics with a critical lens to detect biases and question the status quo.

Recognizing the meaningful links between critical literacy and critical numeracy, we developed a thinking framework to provide a new entry point to mathematics instruction. This framework is intended to be a new way of thinking about mathematics and a new way of doing mathematics. We adapted the *Four Role Resource Model* (Luke & Freebody, 2004), which evolved into the *Four Roles of the Literate Learner* (Ontario Ministry of Education, 2004), to develop the *Four Roles of the Numerate Learner*. The *Four Roles of the Numerate Learner* framework provides a way to approach mathematics with new eyes. The focus is on thinking differently about the way we view mathematics and do mathematics with our students.

The *Four Roles of the Numerate Learner* is a thinking framework that supports effective mathematics instruction and assessment that are differentiated, purposeful, and informed by student learning needs. It is our moral responsibility to deepen our understanding of instructional and assessment strategies that we think will make a difference in improving student thinking and learning. Teaching and learning for *the now* is about making student thinking visible and developing a deeper understanding of concepts. Therefore, we need to create learning conditions that foster critical thinking, risk taking, problem solving, and reflection. Purpose and intentionality are fundamental to current pedagogy as we strive to create supportive and enriching environments that encourage the development of the skills students require to adapt to today's demands. With the support of thinking tools, accountable talk, the gradual release of responsibility, assessment for learning strategies, and differentiated tasks that are integrated and cross-curricular in nature, students can develop abilities to think, express, and reflect—skills for *the now*!

To become numerate, students must learn to *make sense* of the mathematics, *use* mathematical *skills* effectively, *thoughtfully communicate* mathematical thinking, and *critically interpret* mathematical knowledge and skills. The *Four Roles of the Numerate Learner* framework addresses the teaching and learning of mathematics through explicit examples of how each role (sense maker, skill user, thoughtful communicator, and critical interpreter) can support the big ideas in the mathematics curriculum. Focusing on the big ideas gives students the opportunity to link mathematical concepts across the strands and view mathematics as a coherent whole (Charles, 2005). The *Four Roles of the Numerate Learner* framework provides multiple entry points for learners to develop the mathematical concepts and skills required to be numerate. The fundamental intent of this framework is for learners to engage in critical thinking about numeracy.

Unless we, as educators, fully understand the complex roles of the numerate learner, we will be unable to create or foster an environment where students can make sense of mathematics and apply their knowledge and understanding of mathematics to everyday contexts. Our goal is to engage students to not only think critically about mathematics, but also to act on that knowledge to transform a situation. As educators apply the underlying ideas of the *Four Roles of the Numerate Learner* framework as part of their daily practice, students will begin to embrace the underlying principles embedded within the roles and view themselves as numerate learners. As students engage in tasks that support sense making and critical thinking, multiple opportunities for student voice emerge. Students have the opportunity to ask questions, pose problems, explore ideas, and change their thinking about mathematics and the way they see themselves as mathematicians. As we foster and support the integration of these four roles as part of our daily practice, we can be confident that it will enable students to use their diverse identities to build their mathematical knowledge and incorporate their cultural experiences to expand the current dialogue.

By adopting the *Four Roles of the Numerate Learner* framework, students will become skilled critical thinkers, thoughtful problem solvers, and reflective communicators. The notion of critical numeracy is crucial in the teaching and learning process if we want students to be empowered to detect bias and perspective in making sense of their world through mathematics. Moving forward as educators, we need to leverage our instructional and assessment practices to inform our current dialogue and discourse in numeracy. Twenty-first century learning requires teachers and students to adapt to a global world that is changing at an exponential rate. Students need to problem solve, think critically, use higher level thinking skills, and communicate effectively if they are to participate as reflective global citizens in a world of dynamic change. The *Four Roles of the Numerate Learner* framework supports this new way of thinking about the teaching and learning of mathematics.

Reading and Using this Book

This book is designed for educators, school administrators, and those with the responsibility for leading change. It will serve as a guide for planning and implementing improvements in the teaching and learning of mathematics. It is also intended to engage educators in rich conversations about effective mathematics practices.

We begin by describing each of the four roles in the framework, then address each role in detail in subsequent chapters. Each chapter begins with an introduction drawn from our own personal experiences working with educators, administrators, and superintendents, where the focus has been on closing the gap in student achievement in mathematics. These introductions are intended to give the reader a firsthand view of the challenges associated with mathematical thinking and the importance of the *Four Roles of the Numerate Learner* framework. In addition, each chapter provides examples of grade-specific rich tasks and questions for the role, and suggests instructional strategies that support assessment for learning and that are grounded in the thinking framework. Each chapter also includes opportunities for the reader to reflect on how the content presented in the chapter relates to them personally.

Specifically, throughout this book our goals are to:

- provide a description of the *Four Roles of the Numerate Learner* framework;
- unpack critical thinking though the lens of mathematics with a focus on mathematical thinking skills and their alignment to literacy thinking skills;
- embed examples of grade-specific rich mathematics tasks that support the development of the numerate learner;
- offer assessment for learning strategies such as developing learning goals and constructing success criteria;

- provide opportunities for educators to make connections between concepts addressed in the book and the work they are already doing; and
- inspire educators to activate purposeful talk about student learning needs and related teacher learning needs.

Finally, throughout the book, the framework emphasizes student voice with many opportunities for students to ask questions, pose problems, explore ideas, and change their thinking about mathematics and the way they see themselves as mathematicians. This new way of thinking and learning allows learners to engage in critical thinking about numeracy, and ultimately act on this knowledge.

CHAPTER 1

Developing an Understanding of the *Four Roles of the Numerate Learner*

A group of educators in a professional learning community asked a thought-provoking question: How do we teach mathematics for today's learners? We began our journey by exploring the concept of lifelong learning.

Setting the Context

It is the nature of our profession to make constant reference to the idea that we are lifelong learners. But what does this mean? To begin, it is important to define the word *learning*. Educators often engage in professional learning opportunities because we feel the need to learn something new, or perhaps to confirm that current practices are in fact impacting student achievement. However, what is our role as a participant of a professional learning community? What learning is taking place when we bring people together? Having a sense of urgency and a growth mindset are the driving forces of change. If something different is going to happen for students, then it is our moral obligation as educators to reflect on our practices and examine alternate possibilities that are responsive to our students' most urgent learning needs.

"Learning is a permanent change in thinking or behaviour."
Katz, 2013, p. vii

For real change to occur, we also need to understand our students' lives and what makes them excited about learning. How do they learn? What personal and cultural experiences do they bring to the learning? Our students help us shape the curriculum so that teaching and learning are intentional, purposeful, and personalized. Being a lifelong learner means that our thinking is always changing, and we embrace a responsive pedagogy that requires us to be reflective, adaptive, innovative, creative, and collaborative. The journey of lifelong learning begins with knowing our students—their strengths, interests, learning preferences, and learning needs—as well as understanding the elements of cultural competence so that we can implement a curriculum that values diversity and embeds cultural knowledge. Lifelong learning is about being open to trying new practices and reflecting on their impact through evidence of student learning.

Adopting an Inquiry Mindset

At a time when we are paying close attention to mathematics, many questions are emerging about instruction, assessment, differentiation, and integration of cross-curricular skills. How do we disrupt the way we have been teaching mathematics to support our twenty-first century learners? What essential skills do our students need to live in a multi-faceted world? How do we teach mathematical skills and concepts in a way that makes sense for today's learners?

After engaging in professional dialogue with a group of educators, we made the following confirmations that eventually became our guiding principles in moving forward:

- Student thinking and learning are at the forefront of teaching and learning.
- Educators and students need to be presented with opportunities to reflect on their current attitudes and beliefs about what mathematics is and the way we view ourselves as mathematicians.
- Mathematics requires a new way of thinking and doing.
- Mathematics, like language, is the basis for thinking, communicating, and reflecting.
- A cross-curricular and integrated approach is needed if the teaching and learning of mathematics is going to extend beyond the mathematics curriculum to support the development of a numerate learner.
- Differentiation and inclusion are at the heart of meaningful, intentional, and personalized instruction and assessment.

Identifying Connections between Literacy and Numeracy

"(Effective literacy instruction) is about how we communicate in society. It is about social practices and relationships, about knowledge, language, and culture."
Ontario Ministry of Education, 2004, p. ix

We soon realized that effective mathematics instruction is closely linked to effective literacy instruction. If the goal of literacy instruction is to develop a literate learner, then how does effective mathematics instruction support the development of a numerate learner? Are mathematics and numeracy different? And if so, how are they different?

To help us understand the difference between mathematics and numeracy, our conversations took us back to literacy and the fine differences between literacy, new literacies, and critical literacy (see Figure 1.1). Although the columns appear linear, they are conceptually integrated. In addition, it is important to be aware that language is embedded across all literacies.

FIGURE 1.1: COMPARING LITERACY, NEW LITERACIES, AND CRITICAL LITERACY

Literacy	New Literacies	Critical Literacy
"Literacy is defined as the ability to use language and images in rich and varied forms to read, write, listen, speak, view, represent, and think critically about ideas." (Ontario Ministry of Education, 2006)	"As technological convergence develops apace, one needs to combine the skills of critical media literacy with traditional print literacy and new forms of multiple literacies to access and master the new multimedia hypertext environments.	"Critical literacy is not something to be added to the literacy program, but a lens for learning that is an integral part of classroom practice." (Ontario Ministry of Education, 2009) Critical literacy goes one step further than

In literacy, students use all the skills they have learned as they acquire one or multiple languages to engage in thinking, talking, reading, writing, responding to, and reflecting on a wide variety of multi-modal texts.

As students reflect on their thinking, metacognition becomes essential to develop a sense of self-efficacy and self-regulation.

Literacy in this conception involves the abilities to engage effectively in socially-constructed forms of communication and representation." (Kellner, 2000)

"The shift from *literacy* to *literacies* has created possibilities and reconsiderations of pedagogies that look at literacy in multiple ways, through a variety of media and approaches. The term *new literacies* points to multiple linguistic systems within literacy. Literacy practices, which are multiple, shift based on the context, speaker, text, and the function of the literacy event (e.g., doing a Google search)." It's Critical! (Booth, 2008)

"Even definition of the term *text* has gone beyond the traditional acts of reading and writing using an alphabetic code or symbol system, to include digital technology, images, sounds, and oral discourse. Now we refer to a text as a medium with which we make meaning through a variety of modes—written, visual, tactile, or oral. Texts span audio books, magazines, paintings, films, computer screens, narratives, graphics, information, opinions, poetry, songs, scripts, instructions, and procedures. It's Critical!" (Booth, 2008)

basic literacy does, and asks students to question the authority of texts and identify and examine the author's bias or perspective, then engage in dialogue and discourse about text, relating it to their daily lives and their own point of view. It also examines writing as power. Social justice issues are explored and questions are asked such as:
- Whose voice is missing from this text?
- What social action could I take in my school or community as a result of reading this article on environmental stewardship?
- As a global citizen, how do I view this text?

We need to use particular habits of mind to support critical literacy, such as persisting, thinking flexibly, questioning and posing problems, applying past knowledge to new situations, thinking and communicating with clarity and precision, and creating, imagining and innovating. (Costa & Kallick, 2008)

Fiore, Lebar, & Scott-Dunne, 2014

As we worked to unpack the similarities between literacy and numeracy, we examined the definitions of critical literacy as they guided our thinking with respect to numeracy development and what it might mean to be a numerate learner. At the same time, we referred to a similar chart to parallel our thinking on numeracy and critical numeracy (see Figure 1.2).

FIGURE 1.2: COMPARING MATHEMATICAL KNOWLEDGE, NUMERACY, AND CRITICAL NUMERACY

Mathematical Knowledge	Numeracy	Critical Numeracy
Mathematical skills and concepts are used as tools for thinking (reasoning, proving, justifying, reflecting, and communicating).	Numeracy involves using mathematical knowledge to develop an understanding of the role mathematics plays in everyday life. Students apply mathematical skills and concepts to explore and solve practical real-life problems. As students reflect on their mathematical thinking, metacognition becomes essential to develop a sense of self-efficacy and the belief in themselves as successful mathematicians.	"Critical numeracy is a focus on the ways in which practical mathematical situations are implicated in the power relationships and face-to-face politics of everyday life. It is a focus on how numeracy in all its forms is involved in our relationships to each other and the world." (Stoessigner, 2002) Critical numeracy goes one step further than basic numeracy by asking students to question the source(s) of mathematical information (e.g., the notion of using numbers to persuade). Students explore social and political issues and ask questions such as: • How are numbers or shapes being used to support this viewpoint? • Whose numeracy is being advantaged through the presentation of these numbers?

Fiore, Lebar, & Scott-Dunne, 2014

We realized that we could leverage what we know about literacy development to deepen our understanding of mathematics instruction and numeracy development. In addition, we determined that *thinking* and *communicating* are the powerful connections between literacy and numeracy.

The following detailed definition of literacy includes these concepts of thinking and communicating.

> Literacy is . . . "the ability to use language and images in rich and varied forms to read, write, listen, speak, view, represent, and think critically about ideas It involves the capacity to **access**, **manage**, and **evaluate** information; to **think** imaginatively and analytically; and to **communicate** thoughts and ideas effectively. Literacy includes **critical thinking** and **reasoning** to solve problems and make decisions related to issues of **fairness**, **equity**, and **social justice**. Literacy connects individuals and communities and is an **essential** tool for personal growth and active **participation in a cohesive, democratic society**."
>
> Literacy for Learning: The Report of the Expert Panel on Literacy in Grades 4 to 6 in Ontario, *Ontario Ministry of Education, 2004.*

"That is why numeracy—like literacy—is considered so fundamental. Whether the call to action is 'mathematical literacy,' 'quantitative literacy,' 'everyday math,' or 'numeracy,' our challenge as K to 12 educators is to help prepare all our graduates to apply mathematics in the context of their everyday world."
Literacy and Numeracy Secretariat, 2012, p. 1

We determined that the ideas presented in this definition of literacy could easily be used to define numeracy, as indicated below.

> Numeracy is . . . the ability to use mathematical knowledge and skills to think critically about ideas in everyday life. It involves the capacity to **make conjectures** and **interpretations**, **form conclusions**, **evaluate** reasonableness, and **represent** and **justify** solutions; to **think** creatively and analytically; and to **communicate** thoughts, ideas, and solutions logically. Numeracy includes **critical thinking** and **reasoning** to solve problems, make sense of mathematical concepts, and question issues of **fairness**, **equity** and **social justice**. Numeracy connects individuals and communities and is an essential tool for personal growth and active **participation in a cohesive**, **democratic society**.

Aligning Effective Literacy and Numeracy Practices

Thinking is an integral component of literacy development. As a result, to prepare students for today's world, making student thinking visible needs to be the underlying goal of every teaching and learning experience. Figure 1.3 outlines the instructional and assessment actions that will help make thinking visible across the curriculum. They are interdisciplinary in nature and align literacy to numeracy.

FIGURE 1.3: INTEGRATION OF INSTRUCTION AND ASSESSMENT

Begin with the students as personal and cultural resources
• Assess students' already acquired knowledge and experiences.   • Get to know students' interests, learning preferences, and natural curiosities.
Implement comprehensive/balanced instruction using the gradual release of responsibility
• Based on evidence gathered from observations, conversations, and products, decide which instructional approach students primarily require at any given time to support identified learning needs (e.g., *modelled, shared, guided,* or *independent* practice).

Use assessment *for, as, of* learning

- Know the intended learning outcomes and different purposes for gathering evidence during the learning process.
- Use assessment *for* learning to improve student learning and as the basis for providing descriptive feedback (emphasize developing learning goals and co-constructing success criteria to describe successful attainment of intended learning).
- Use assessment *as* learning to help students develop metacognitive practices to monitor their own learning and develop goals for improving learning.
- Use assessment *of* learning for the purpose of evaluation.

Adapted from Growing Success – Assessment, Evaluation, and Reporting in Ontario Schools, *Ontario Ministry of Education, 2010.*

Use accountable talk

- Use accountable talk strategies, such as turn and talk, wait time, paraphrasing (e.g., *Who can repeat what _____ just said?*), re-voicing (*I think that I am hearing you say that . . .*), adding on (*Tell me more about that. Why do you think that?*).
- Provide opportunities for students to engage in intentional, focused talk about a specific topic where they can deliberate, exchange ideas, ask questions, check understanding, defend opinions, draw conclusions, explain their thinking, make connections, and justify.

Adapted from West, Metamorphosis Teaching Learning Communities, *http://www.metamorphosistlc. com.*

Promote inquiry-based and problem-based learning

- Create classroom learning conditions and spaces that foster wonderings and curiosities.
- Provide authentic learning opportunities where students are required to use skills to ask questions, think, problem solve, resolve doubts, and find the truth.

Adapted from IQ – A Practical Guide to Inquiry-Based Learning, *Watt & Colyer, 2014.*

Adopt a three-part lesson mindset

- Activate student thinking.
- Develop student thinking.
- Consolidate student thinking.

Adapted from Asking Effective Questions, *Literacy and Numeracy Secretariat, 2011.*

Provide thinking tools and engaging texts

- Encourage students to use a range of manipulatives as thinking tools that support knowledge construction through exploration, investigation, discovery, and creation.
- Provide students with choice to select from a range of engaging texts, including literary, informational, and graphic, to develop essential thinking skills (e.g., *inferring, interpreting, extending understanding, analyzing, evaluating, synthesizing*).

Create rich tasks and authentic learning experiences

- Develop learning tasks/experiences that promote student thinking, problem solving, and decision making, and that help students adopt a critical stance about the world they live in.

Foster a responsive learning environment

- Adapt and adjust instruction "in the moment" to respond to students' specific learning needs.

We can use these instructional and assessment practices to implement a new thinking framework to support the teaching and learning of mathematics. The responsive and adaptive nature of these practices promotes learning spaces shaped by students' strengths, needs, and interests. They provoke a differentiated and flexible learning environment that fosters curiosity about instructional and assessment strategies, intended to develop deep mathematical understanding and thinking of concepts and skills.

Developing a New Thinking Framework in Mathematics

"Literacy in the twenty-first century involves not a single skill but a complex combination of skills and resources that the literate learner draws upon to make meaning from texts of many types."
Ontario Ministry of Education, 2006, p. 28

Dr. Allan Luke and Peter Freebody (1990) developed the *Four Resources Model* several decades ago, which subsequently evolved into the *Four Roles of the Literate Learner* framework. This evolving literacy framework focuses on guiding literacy instruction, selecting resources, and implementing the practices required for students to learn a repertoire of complex literacy skills. We used this model to develop a similar framework for numeracy. The *Four Roles of the Numerate Learner* framework supports an integrated approach to effective mathematics instruction that makes sense and fosters mathematical thinking that promotes numeracy development (Fiore, Lebar, & Scott-Dunne, 2014). Our framework builds on educators' understanding of how to effectively teach mathematics, while considering the mathematical practices that students need to learn to construct mathematical knowledge, become mathematicians, and engage with mathematics.

The *Four Roles of the Literate Learner* framework was not intended to focus on a particular teaching method, pedagogical style, or preference (Comber, 1997). Rather, its central goal was to integrate the kinds of practices students need to learn in today's new economies and cultures (Freebody & Luke, 1999). Figure 1.4 provides an outline of the model.

FIGURE 1.4: THE *FOUR ROLES OF THE LITERATE LEARNER* FRAMEWORK

	Meaning Maker	Code User	
What is the text about? What is the author's message?	Uses prior knowledge and personal and/or world experiences to construct and communicate meaning when reading, writing, speaking, listening, viewing, and representing. The literate learner is a "text participant" forming and communicating their own interpretation in light of their own knowledge and point of view.	Recognizes and uses the features and structures of written, visual, and multi-modal texts, including the alphabet, sounds in words, phonemic awareness, phonics, spelling, conventions, sentence structure, text organization, and graphics, as well as other visual and non-visual cues to break the "code" of texts.	How is this word similar to others you know? Why are these words bolded?
	The Literate Learner		
	Text User	Text Analyzer	
What type of text is this? How do you know? Why is this text form effective for this purpose and audience?	Understands that purpose and audience help to determine the way text is constructed: form, format, medium, structure, tone, the degree of formality, and sequence of components. The literate learner uses this knowledge and a variety of thinking processes to read, listen, and view, as well as to write, speak, and represent ideas.	Understands that texts are not neutral; that they represent particular views, beliefs, values, and perspectives to serve different interests; that other views and perspectives may be missing; that the design and messages of texts can be interpreted, critiqued, challenged, and alternatives considered. The literate learner decides what to think now, considers possibilities and when to take action.	Whose voice is represented? Whose voice is missing? What does the author want me to believe and/or think?

Adapted from Literacy for Learning: The Report of the Expert Panel on Literacy in Grades 4–6 in Ontario, *Ontario Ministry of Education, 2004 and* The Four Resources Model, *Freebody & Luke, 1990. Created for Peel District School Board's* Monograph – Comprehensive Literacy – Moving Forward, *2013.*

Using the thinking around each practice in the *Four Roles of the Literate Learner*, we started to unpack each of the four roles for the *Four Roles of the Numerate Learner* framework. Much time was spent reflecting on the purpose and functionality behind each practice and how the thinking might be transferred to the dimensions of mathematics. We considered that students' existing mathematical knowledge and cultural and social experiences could help develop a critical lens for how students learn and do mathematics (Freebody & Luke, 1999). Our goal was to develop a thinking framework that could provide multiple entry points into a new world of approaching mathematics instruction—a new way of thinking and learning.

Like the *Four Roles of the Literate Learner*, the *Four Roles of the Numerate Learner* framework is not intended to be linear or hierarchical. The roles are interconnected and support integrative thinking and differentiated instruction for learners who have diverse learning needs at any given time. The intent is for learners to engage in critical thinking about numeracy (Fiore, Lebar, & Scott-Dunne, 2014). Figure 1.5 outlines the model.

FIGURE 1.5: THE *FOUR ROLES OF THE NUMERATE LEARNER* FRAMEWORK

Sense Maker	Skill User
Makes sense of mathematical patterns, operations, computations, procedures, relationships, and language. *A sense maker* applies knowledge and understanding of mathematical concepts to a variety of contexts. *Developing and consolidating procedural fluency and a conceptual understanding* • Does this answer make sense to you? • What is this question asking you to do? What words or phrases make you think that? • Where have you seen this before? • How would you represent the data? (e.g., numerically, geometrically, algebraically, pictorially, graphically) • How can we represent this in a different way? • How do these representations (e.g., numeric, geometric, algebraic, pictorial, graphical) compare? How are they different? • What are the similarities and differences between these two numbers? • What is the pattern? How do you know?	Recognizes and knows when and how to apply number operations, computational strategies, and procedures. A *skill user* uses mathematical conventions and vocabulary to express and organize ideas and mathematical thinking. *Developing procedural fluency* • What does that word mean? (e.g., sum, product, ratio, mean, median, mode) • What patterns do you see? • Which number is bigger? • What mathematical operation are you going to use? • Determine the value of the variable. • Simplify the expression. • How many ways can you represent $1.50? • Organize data into categories (e.g., based on qualities such as colour or favourite food). • How do we represent parallel lines? • How can you represent equal line segments?

Thought Communicator	Critical interpreter
Communicates mathematical thinking through problem solving, reasoning and proving, reflecting, using thinking tools, connecting, and representing to gain a deeper understanding of mathematical concepts. • Explain how you would find the 10th term of the pattern and justify your answer. • Can you share and explain the results of the survey you designed? • Select and justify the unit that you think should be used to measure the perimeter. • Here is the answer. What could the question be? Justify your response. • Given these two different solutions, determine which solution is correct and explain your thinking. • Provide a counter-example to represent your thinking. • How does your solution compare and contrast to your partner's? • Create a poem, song, or dance to demonstrate your understanding.	Adopts a critical numeracy lens to apply mathematical knowledge and skills to challenge the power in the usage of numbers, patterns, measurements, graphs, shapes, figures, pictures, and/or statistics (e.g., using a critical numeracy lens in practical situations to examine the role mathematics plays in the world and the bias and perspective of those using the numeracy). • Who might benefit from using these numbers in this context? • Can I use data to support my argument or illustrate my ideas? • Can I use data to support my critical stance? • Can I use mathematical knowledge to question data? (e.g., biased statistics on child poverty) • Is the mathematical thinking represented fairly? Are there other perspectives that need to be considered? • Identify the bias in this representation of data.

Adapted from The Four Roles of the Numerate Learner, *Fiore, Lebar, & Scott-Dunne, 2014.*

Skill User

Having knowledge of number operations and computational strategies is necessary but not sufficient if we want students to begin to make sense of mathematical concepts. A *skill user* demonstrates procedural fluency, which incorporates basic facts, number operations, computational strategies, and procedures such as simplifying, solving, and evaluating. The acquisition of such knowledge and skills is an important focus of the mathematics curriculum as it supports a balanced mathematics program (Fiore, Lebar, & Scott-Dunne, 2014).

Sense Maker

Students begin to make sense of mathematics when they are immersed in a culture of mathematical learning that deepens their procedural knowledge and conceptual understanding of mathematical concepts. To promote the role of *sense maker*, educators create learning experiences that foster the development of skills such as exploring, investigating, reflecting, analyzing, justifying, reasoning, interpreting, and drawing conclusions. They also make connections to enhance students' sense of mathematical patterns, operations, computations, procedures, relationships, conventions, and use of language to consolidate their understanding.

Thought Communicator

Students deepen their procedural knowledge and conceptual understanding of mathematical concepts when they are provided with opportunities to communicate their mathematical thinking. In order to make this thinking visible, students must engage in meaningful mathematics discussions where they are not only sharing ideas, but also building on others' opinions. A *thought communicator* challenges the ideas of others by applying metacognitive knowledge to reflect on their own thinking and the thinking of others through effective questioning. Students understand what it means to engage in different types of thinking by co-constructing success criteria with the teacher that describe what a particular kind of thinking looks like as they experience it. As their understanding of various types of thinking is developed, such as reasoning and proving, justifying, analyzing, inferring, interpreting, and connecting, students are then able to communicate their thinking about mathematical ideas to enhance their understanding of concepts.

Critical Interpreter

As students make sense of the mathematical concepts, they need to adopt a critical stance, an attitude or a way of viewing the world. Being critically numerate is about using mathematical knowledge and numeracy skills to disrupt commonly held assumptions and consider multiple viewpoints to better understand the world and how it is perceived. A *critical interpreter* asks questions that challenge attitudes, beliefs, biases, and perspectives that may lie beneath the surface of mathematical ideas, information represented in graphs and tables, usage of numbers, patterns, measurements, shapes, figures, pictures, and/or statistics. Students examine relationships of power that may be presented through the use of language, data, representations of mathematical thinking, justifications, and the process of forming judgments and conclusions from mathematical ideas.

An Opportunity for Reflection

Think about the *Four Roles of the Numerate Learner* as a thinking framework and consider how you might begin to use it to support mathematics instruction and assessment.

Why Does this Framework Matter?

Unless we fully understand the complex roles of the numerate learner, we will be unable to create or foster an environment where students can make sense of mathematics, apply it to everyday contexts, and use it to question numbers, patterns, measurements, graphs, shapes, figures, pictures, and/or statistics in their world. Our goal in using this framework is to engage students to not only think critically about mathematics, but to act on this knowledge to transform a situation.

As principals encourage students and teachers to become familiar with these four roles, there are multiple opportunities for student voice. Students have the opportunity to ask questions, pose problems, explore ideas, and change their thinking about mathematics and the way they see themselves as mathematicians. As we foster and support the integration of these four roles as part of our daily practice, we can be confident that students will be able to use their diverse identities to build their mathematical knowledge and incorporate their cultural experiences to expand the current dialogue (Fiore, Lebar, & Scott-Dunne, 2014).

Using Responsive Instruction

"Teachers' adaptability is honed by constant reflection: They enter each lesson with a clear plan to successfully teach a concept in a differentiated manner, but they are also ready to adapt if their best-laid plans are not sufficient for every child."
Parsons et al., 2013, p. 42

Responsive teaching involves responding to student learning needs and adapting instruction during the teaching and learning process. It requires us to adjust our instruction in real-time to meet the specific learning needs of individual students or the demands of the situation in which we find ourselves (Fairbanks et al., 2010; Parsons, 2012). This way of thinking supports a differentiated learning environment that connects educators to learners' strengths, needs, and interests, and involves making adaptations that were not or could not be anticipated (Parsons et al., 2013). Thoughtful adaptations require on-going observations and monitoring of student learning so that immediate adjustments can be made to instruction, the learning environment, and student tasks. Evidence of student learning consistently informs educators of where students need to go in their learning journey. Using assessment for learning practices creates learning conditions that foster risk taking, independence, student efficacy, success, and shared responsibility for learning.

The *Four Roles of the Numerate Learner* framework provides a responsive approach to effective mathematics instruction. The framework places the learner at the centre of the learning process and informs intentional instruction that supports students' diverse learning needs. The four roles are not sequential and represent a fluid, adaptive, and flexible approach to the teaching and learning of mathematics. This thinking framework represents the fabric for mathematical learning that has multiple threads, our students, weaving their way through the various roles in order to combine and integrate a repertoire of skills to become critical thinkers, thoughtful communicators, and meaning makers.

Numeracy as an Interdisciplinary Approach

It is critical to approach thinking skills from a cross-curricular and integrated lens, as they permeate all curricular areas. We all need to be teachers of literacy! By using an interdisciplinary planning process, we can think about the big ideas that students need to *know*, the skills that they need to apply (*do*), and the attitudes that are required to *be* active citizens (Drake & Reid, 2010). Having an interdisciplinary lens means that we are approaching the curriculum from an inquiry mindset to uncover the big ideas/enduring understandings and make cross-curricular connections, instead of simply covering specific expectations and isolated skills and concepts. By connecting ideas and skills from different subject areas, we are "providing students with multiple learning opportunities to reinforce and demonstrate their knowledge and skills in a range of settings" (Literacy and Numeracy Secretariat, 2010, p. 5).

Consider the following example. Two big ideas in the mathematics curriculum for data management and probability are collection and organization of data and data relationships (Ontario Ministry of Education, 2005). Specifically, "by the end of Grade 5 students will collect and organize discrete or continuous primary data and secondary data and display the data using charts and graphs, including broken-line graphs" (p. 84). By adopting an interdisciplinary or integrated approach, we can think about how ideas, concepts, and skills from other curricular areas could support the teaching and learning of this mathematics concept (*knowing*). From a reading perspective, students need to learn how to read, infer, and interpret information from graphic text features, such as graphs, charts, tables, maps, etc. So we now are reflecting on reading and comprehension skills that students will need to apply (*doing*) in order to make sense of the charts and graphs in mathematics.

A further cross-disciplinary connection would be to connect the mathematical skills of collecting, organizing, and interpreting data to the social studies curriculum, which requires students to learn how to "extract information from and constructing various types of graphs, including line, bar, and scatter graphs related to various topics" (Ontario Ministry of Education, 2013, p. 48). As students are acquiring the knowledge about collecting and organizing data and applying the skills of reading, inferring, and interpreting data, they are fostering the notion of *being*. Students are also critically thinking about the relationships between data sets and effectively communicating their ideas as they are attempting to make sense of the learning.

To further support integration and planning from an interdisciplinary view, we reflected on how the literacy thinking skills could connect to the development of mathematical thinking. For example, how might understanding the skills of *inferring, interpreting, analyzing, evaluating, synthesizing,* and *examining biases* in literacy support thinking in mathematics? To deepen our understanding of how these skills could be used to leverage mathematical thinking, we needed to deconstruct the thinking skills in the mathematics curriculum in order to build our understanding of numeracy development. As a result, we can begin to see ourselves as teachers of numeracy while adopting an integrated mindset.

The Role of *Thinking* in the *Four Roles of the Numerate Learner*

Thinking is at the heart of the *Four Roles of the Numerate Learner* framework.

An Opportunity for Reflection

What do you mean when you use the word *think*? How do your students interpret the word *think*?

What is *Thinking*?

Our goal is to nurture learners so that they have the power to be active participants in a democratic society. Thinking, therefore, is the underpinning of all teaching and learning experiences. If we were to take the Oxford Dictionary definition of *thinking* as "the process of considering or reasoning about something"

(2015), then what would this look like in the context of literacy and numeracy development? The Ontario Ministry of Education (2012) describes *thinking* as the ability to "access, manage, create, and evaluate information in order to think imaginatively and critically to solve problems and make decisions, including those related to issues of fairness, equity, and social justice" (p. 12). The latter part of this definition introduces the element of "critical" thought. Critical thinking is about reasoning so that we can make sound decisions about what to believe and/ or what to do (Brookhart, 2010).

An Opportunity for Reflection

Is the critical thinking that students need to do to be literate similar or different from the critical thinking required to be numerate? Explain how you think they are similar and/or different.

What is *Thinking* in Literacy?

"Clearly the word *think* plays an astonishingly prominent role in our speech and writing. If one considers just verbs, Oxford Dictionary rates the word *think* as the twelfth most used verb in the English Language. When we use the word *think*, what meaning do those listening to us infer? When we tell someone we are *thinking*, what is it we are actually doing? Although no data is available, one might expect the word *think* to occur even more frequently in classrooms. When teachers use the word *think*, what do they intend? When students hear it, how do they interpret it? Does it lead to any actions on their part?"
Ritchhart, Church, & Morrison, 2011, p. 5

If student learning and understanding are the intended outcomes, and we believe that learning is the product of thinking, then we need to promote the alignment of instructional and assessment strategies to support student thinking (Ritchhart, Church, & Morrison, 2011). To begin this learning process, we can closely examine language and mathematics curricula through the lens of thinking and critical thinking to uncover connections. By reflecting on what students are expected to know, understand, and do, we can develop a deeper understanding of the thought processes needed to be a literate learner.

To help make student thinking visible and plan for learning experiences that foster thinking, we unpacked each of the thinking skills: *analyzing, evaluating, synthesizing,* and *identifying points of view and examining biases.* Our goal was to develop a common understanding to guide students in co-constructing success criteria that would then be used to monitor learning and the development of each skill. To support thinking, students need to develop an understanding and apply literacy/thinking skills in a cross-curricular and integrated manner, as shown in Figure 1.6.

FIGURE 1.6: LITERACY THINKING SKILLS

Students need to ...

- make inferences and interpretations
- extend understanding by connecting, comparing, and contrasting
- summarize
- analyze
- evaluate
- synthesize
- identify points of view and examine biases
- question and challenge commonly held assumptions related to authority, power, and language
- use metacognitive practices to reflect on learning and thinking

---

Ontario Ministry of Education, 2006

What is *Analyzing*?

When deconstructing *analyzing* as a higher-order thinking skill, we need to think about the learning goal and what students are expected to learn. Consider the learning goal for *analyzing* as learning how to break down the components of a text by identifying each part, describing the function of each part, and explaining the relationship between parts and why the author/creator of the text chose to include the identified parts, as well as explaining how they contribute to the overall meaning and understanding of a text (Anderson et al., 2001). Figure 1.7 shows the success criteria developed to guide instruction and assessment of *analyzing*.

FIGURE 1.7: SUCCESS CRITERIA FOR *ANALYZING*

> **I can . . .**
>
> - locate key words from the text and explain why the author chose these words
> - take apart a story and explain how each part helps me understand what the author is trying to tell me (e.g., *message*)
> - name the text form and explain how it supports the author's purpose for writing
> - explain why the author chose to use a particular text feature, image, language feature to help me understand the message
> - identify text features and how they might support the overall meaning of a text
> - explain why the author chose certain elements (e.g., *name the elements appropriate to grade level*) to create meaning
> - explain how word choice helps create meaning and achieve a certain purpose
> - name different graphics used in a text (e.g., *diagram, photograph, illustration*) and explain why the author chose to include them to help create meaning
> - infer the choices an author makes about how a text is organized and structured

Developed by Maria Luisa Lebar for the Peel District School Board, 2013.

What is *Evaluating*?

Consider the learning goal for *evaluating* as learning how to assess and make a judgment about something by assigning quality, significance, or worth to it based on established criteria (Anderson et al., 2001). Figure 1.8 shows the success criteria developed to guide instruction and assessment of *evaluating*.

FIGURE 1.8: SUCCESS CRITERIA FOR *EVALUATING*

> **I can . . .**
>
> - use co-created criteria to assess how effective a title is for a text and its intended purpose (e.g., *I think the title is a good choice because . . .; students refer to constructed criteria to explain thinking*)
> - use co-constructed criteria to respond to the different parts of a story/text (e.g., *Are the characters suitable, appropriate, effective? Is the setting effective? Are the images in the informational text appropriate, suitable?*)
> - express my feelings about what I have read and support my thinking with reasons and evidence that are based on co-created criteria
> - provide an opinion about a text or parts of a text and use supporting evidence to justify my thinking (e.g., *I think that this is a good narrative because . . .; students determine if the narrative is good or not based on criteria that were developed for a "good narrative"; students need to know what makes a good narrative before making a judgment about it*)

- express my thoughts about how well written a text is and how well the author gets his/her message across (e.g., *What is the structure of the text? How effectively do the components of the text convey a message? Narrative: setting, characters, problem, solution; students need to understand the structure of a text form and think about the effectiveness of the components, use of language, text features, literary devices*)
- express an opinion about how useful the text features are in helping me understand the text
- explain how I know that a text is non-fiction (*informational*) by using evidence such as text features, illustrations, word choice, etc.

Developed by Maria Luisa Lebar for the Peel District School Board, 2013.

What is *Synthesizing*?

Consider the learning goal for *synthesizing* as learning how to connect, integrate, and combine information and ideas about a text in order to arrive at a new understanding of it (Ontario Ministry of Education, 2006). Figure 1.9 shows the success criteria developed to guide instruction and assessment of *synthesizing*.

FIGURE 1.9: SUCCESS CRITERIA FOR *SYNTHESIZING*

I can...

- use my "schema" or background knowledge to think about what I already know as I am trying to understand and make sense of what I am reading/viewing (e.g., *students use a "coding the text" strategy to mark the parts of the text already known; students code the new parts and think about how what is already known, in combination with the new parts, can create a new understanding*)
- build on my understanding of a text by looking closely at the different parts, such as pictures, word choice, text features, etc., and how they help create meaning
- notice parts of a text that stand out and infer what they might mean, such as illustrations, print features (*font size, bold print*), text features (*captions, headings*)
- explain how my thinking changes or evolves (grows) as I read/view and get more information (e.g., *I now understand ... because ...*)
- talk about the part of the text where my thinking changed
- think about how a text is organized and how the different parts work together to create a message (e.g., *components of a narrative, report, procedure, persuasive, explanation*)

Developed by Maria Luisa Lebar for the Peel District School Board, 2013.

What is *Identifying Points of View and Examining Biases*?

Consider the learning goal for *identifying points of view/biases* as understanding that texts represent particular views, beliefs, values, and perspectives to serve different interests; that other views and perspectives may be missing; and that the design and messages of texts can be interpreted, critiqued, challenged, and alternatives considered (Luke and Freebody, 1990). Figure 1.10 shows the success criteria developed to guide instruction and assessment of *identifying points of view and examining biases*.

FIGURE 1.10: SUCCESS CRITERIA FOR *IDENTIFYING POINTS OF VIEW AND EXAMINING BIASES*

> **I can . . .**
>
> - identify/state a point of view from the text and explain my thinking by using evidence from the text
> - identify/state another/alternate point of view and justify my thinking by providing evidence
> - talk about strategies that the author uses to make people believe certain things
> - identify what the author is representing in a text (what is there) and what is missing (e.g., *Whose voice is missing? Who is not represented?*)
> - explain how the author uses language and images to make me think in a certain way
> - talk about/explain how a text might be different if it was told by someone else (another point of view)
> - share my thinking about whether the text is fair or not using supporting evidence
> - talk about/explain how a text might be different if told in another time or place

Developed by Maria Luisa Lebar for the Peel District School Board, 2013.

What is Mathematical Thinking?

It is important that we are explicit about what we mean by *mathematical thinking* if we are going to make students' thinking visible in our classrooms. Figure 1.11 provides a list of mathematical thinking skills.

FIGURE 1.11: MATHEMATICAL THINKING SKILLS

> **Students need to ...**
>
> - estimate
> - evaluate (make judgments)
> - form conclusions
> - infer
> - reason
> - prove
> - justify
> - make convincing arguments
> - connect
> - reflect
> - solve problems
> - classify
> - recognize relationships
> - hypothesize
> - offer opinions with reasons

Ontario Ministry of Education, 2005

It is evident that the mathematical thinking skills (from Figure 1.11) are directly linked to the literacy thinking skills previously noted (presented in Figure 1.6). We then co-constructed the learning goals and success criteria for *reasoning and proving, connecting*, and *reflecting*. These mathematical thinking skills are embedded in the *Four Roles of the Numerate Learner* framework. For example, students need to

- reason, prove, connect, reflect, and justify in order to make sense of the mathematical concepts and relationships in the role of "sense maker";
- use mathematical conventions and vocabulary to apply skills in the role of "skill user";
- communicate their thinking through the role of "thought communicator"; and
- adopt a critical stance to consider multiple mathematical perspectives and examine assumptions, biases, and issues of power that may be represented in mathematical information, data, or statistics.

"When we make thinking visible, we get not only a window into what students understand but also how they are understanding it. Uncovering students' thinking gives us evidence of students' insights as well as their misconceptions. We need to make thinking visible because it provides us with the information we as teachers need to plan opportunities that will take students' learning to the next level and enable continued engagement with the ideas being explored. It is only when we understand what our students are thinking, feeling, and attending to that we can use that knowledge to further engage and support them in the process of understanding."
Ritchhart, Church, & Morrison, 2011, p. 27

28

What is *Reasoning and Proving*?

Consider the learning goal for *reasoning and proving* as learning how to explore, gather evidence, develop ideas, make conjectures, and justify results. Figure 1.12 shows the success criteria developed to guide instruction and assessment of *reasoning and proving*.

FIGURE 1.12: SUCCESS CRITERIA FOR *REASONING AND PROVING*

I can . . .

- make a reasonable guess
- use models to infer and draw conclusions
- justify my thinking by reasoning with evidence (e.g., *Explain how you came to a solution and why you think you are right.*)
- present proof that supports my argument

Adapted from TIPS4RM: Mathematical Process, *Ontario Ministry of Education, n.d.*

What is *Connecting*?

Consider the learning goal for *connecting* as learning how to make connections between strategies, concepts within the strands, previous learning and experiences to new learning, and mathematics to other subject areas. Figure 1.13 shows the success criteria developed to guide instruction and assessment of *connecting*.

FIGURE 1.13: SUCCESS CRITERIA FOR *CONNECTING*

I can . . .

- apply a strategy that extends previous learning to a new context
- make connections between mathematical concepts between strands
- apply mathematical concepts to other subject areas
- make connections between different representations
- make connections between different strategies

Adapted from TIPS4RM: Mathematical Process, *Ontario Ministry of Education, n.d.*

What is *Reflecting*?

Consider the learning goal for *reflecting* as learning how to make sense of the problem and reflect on and monitor their own thought and learning process. Figure 1.14 shows the success criteria developed to guide instruction and assessment of *reflecting*.

FIGURE 1.14: SUCCESS CRITERIA FOR *REFLECTING*

I can . . .

- apply and extend knowledge to new contexts (e.g., *How does this compare to . . .?*)
- think about the reasonableness (e.g., *Does this answer make sense to you?*)
- verify a solution to a problem by using a different strategy
- use a different strategy to solve a problem (e.g., *How else could you show your thinking?*)
- select the most effective strategy to provide a solution to the task

Adapted from TIPS4RM: Mathematical Process, *Ontario Ministry of Education, n.d.*

Making Thinking Visible: Unpacking *Justifying*

To make thinking visible, students need to understand the purpose for a specific type of thinking and what it would look like when it is applied in various learning contexts. For example, consider *justifying* as a critical thinking skill that supports *reasoning and proving* in mathematics. What does it mean to *justify* your thinking? Fiore and Lebar (2015) state, "*Justifying* asks 'why' and 'how'. When *justifying*, one is proving with evidence that is reasonable and logical. Educators can reinforce *justifying* by asking open-ended questions that require their students to explain *how* they came to a solution, and *why* they think that they are right. In order for students to learn how to *justify*, they need to understand and apply a range of processing skills. These would include making inferences, interpreting, analyzing, evaluating, synthesizing, and detecting bias." The literacy connection becomes apparent!

Fiore and Lebar (2015) further state, "The teaching and learning of *evaluating* will undoubtedly support the development of *justification* as an integral thinking skill in mathematics. *Justifying* requires students to assess the effectiveness of the evidence before the evidence can be used to support their thinking—the skill of evaluating. When assigning quality to evidence, it is important to co-construct criteria for reasonableness and logical reasoning. For example, students asked to think about whether a title is a good choice for a text need to understand and use the criteria for what makes an effective title. Only with this prior understanding can the student explain the **why**—why the title in question is effective or ineffective."

An Opportunity for Reflection

To deepen your understanding of the mathematical thinking skills, select one skill from Figure 1.11 and create success criteria similar to those developed for *reasoning and proving*, *connecting*, and *reflecting*.

We often ask our students to explain their thinking, yet many educators struggle with what it actually means to deconstruct thinking. Inevitably, the assessment of students' mathematical thinking becomes a daunting task. It is only when students make their mathematical thinking visible, through the purposeful use of rich mathematics tasks, that we can properly assess their understanding, provide descriptive feedback, and consequently improve student learning.

Attributes of Mathematical Thinking

Mathematical thinking can be described as a series of attributes (see Figure 1.15) that emerge from the thinking skills outlined in Figure 1.11 (Fiore & Lebar, 2015).

"What is required are teachers who are aware of what individual students are thinking and knowing, and who can construct meaning and meaningful experiences in light of this knowledge."
Hattie, 2009, p. 36

"The thinking process supports a deeper understanding of concepts with a focus on students being able to make sense of the knowledge and skills outlined in the curriculum. The essence of every teaching and learning experience in a classroom is to make student thinking visible in order to ensure students have a deep understanding of concepts. A deep understanding—conceptual understanding—of mathematics occurs when students are able to make connections, see relationships, and more importantly, make sense of them."
Fiore & Lebar, 2015, p. 22

FIGURE 1.15: ATTRIBUTES OF MATHEMATICAL THINKING

Students need to ...

- look for a pattern and make generalizations
- make connections and recognize relationships
- identify and incorporate appropriate mathematical knowledge and skills needed to solve a problem
- see mathematics as a connected whole
- make sense of the mathematics
- reflect
- reason with evidence (e.g., *justify*)
- explain, interpret, and draw conclusions

An Opportunity for Reflection

Describe a task you have used that supported the development of students' mathematical thinking. How did you assess students' mathematical thinking during the performance of the task?

Thinking is an integral component of the mathematics curricula and central to teaching and learning in the twenty-first century—*the now*. Thinking is brought about through purposeful and intentional teaching with the support of thinking tools, purposeful talk, a repertoire of instructional and assessment actions, and rich tasks (Fiore & Lebar, 2015). Environments that support the development of students' mathematical thinking have the potential to increase students' mathematical conceptual understanding, creativity, and confidence, and change the way they think about mathematics and the way they see themselves as mathematicians.

Looking Forward

In the following chapters, we closely unpack each of the four roles: *skill user, sense maker, thought communicator,* and *critical interpreter* by explaining the purpose and function of each practice and how they can deepen our understanding of mathematics instruction and contribute to the development of a numerate learner. We provide examples of tasks for each role, at various grade levels and divisions, to demonstrate how educators can target the learning and thinking by strategically designing tasks that connect mathematical content knowledge and thinking through the lens of the *Four Roles of the Numerate Learner* framework. The tasks are intended to guide our thinking about creating learning opportunities and spaces that engage students in purposeful mathematical learning that is intentional, responsive, meaningful, collaborative, creative, and that foster critical thought. As examples, the tasks emphasize the importance of developing and applying integrated and interconnected skills and concepts as students become numerate learners.

Using Rich Tasks as a Bridge between Assessment and Instruction

"Through formative assessment, students develop a clear understanding of learning targets and receive feedback that helps them to improve. In addition, by applying formative strategies such as asking strategic effective questions, providing students with immediate feedback, and engaging students in self-reflection, teachers receive evidence of students' reasoning and misconceptions to use in adjusting instruction. By receiving formative feedback, students learn how to assess themselves and how to improve their own learning. At the core of formative assessment is an understanding of the influence that assessment has on student motivation and the need for students to actively monitor and engage in their learning. The use of formative assessment has been shown to result in higher achievement."
NCTM, 2013, p.1

Focusing on assessment *for* learning—formative assessment—produces a substantial increase in student achievement (Black & Wiliam, 1998). The following five strategies support effective assessment (Wiliam, 2011):

- Clarifying, sharing, and understanding learning intentions and success criteria.
- Eliciting evidence of learners' achievement through the use of effective classroom discussion, questions, activities, and tasks.
- Providing feedback that moves learning forward.
- Activating students as instructional resources for one another.
- Activating students as owners of their own learning.

Through the lens of mathematics, formative assessment can be described as a process that incorporates the purposeful use of rich tasks, supports sense making, and enhances students' mathematical thinking. Formative assessment is an opportunity to reflect on the learning, based on clearly established success criteria linked to a learning goal, and respond to the learning through descriptive and immediate feedback to help students improve. Teachers and students are viewed as co-learners through this process.

Conversations about assessment and instruction are often kept separated. In reality, it is impossible to set the two apart if we are going to enhance students' mathematical thinking. As a result, rich tasks are the bridge between assessment and instruction. When used purposefully as an instructional strategy, rich tasks provide us with the opportunity to gather evidence of students' thinking and learning, along with students' opportunities to communicate their mathematical thinking as they make sense of mathematical concepts. We are then presented with opportunities to assess student learning and plan next steps.

An Opportunity for Reflection

Reflecting on our beliefs about instruction and assessment is a critical component of the teaching and learning process. Complete the survey in Appendix C as you reflect on effective instructional actions to support sense making.

Putting it all Together

The following rich tasks support the role of sense maker in effective mathematics practices and enhance students' mathematical thinking.

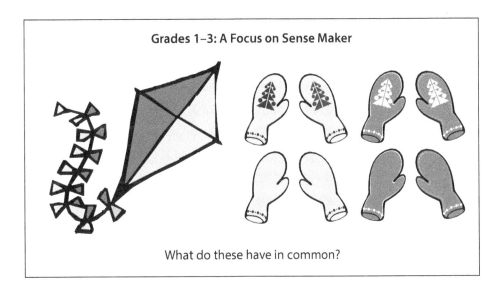

Grades 1–3: A Focus on Sense Maker

What do these have in common?

Learning Goal

Students will learn that the fraction $\frac{1}{2}$ can mean half of a single area or $\frac{1}{2}$ of the items in a group. As a result, they will understand that they need to know what the whole is to make a fraction meaningful.

How does this task support the role of sense maker? The task:

- has a curricular focus;
- provides opportunities for connections;
- is grounded in problem solving;
- focuses on conceptual understanding; and
- engages students in mathematical thinking.

Success Criteria

I can …

- describe fractions as parts of a set
- describe that the digit in the denominator indicates the number of items that are in one part of the set, and the digit in the numerator indicates the number of items that are in the other part of the set in part-part relationships
- describe fractions as parts of a whole
- describe that the digit in the denominator indicates the number of equal digits in part-whole relationships
- describe fractions as a single number
- describe a fraction as a relationship between a part and a part or as a part to a whole

Learning Goal

Students will learn to determine dimensions of length and width given a perimeter so that they can explain how to describe an object using different measurements.

How does this task support the role of sense maker? The task:

- has a curricular focus;
- provides opportunities for connections;
- is grounded in problem solving;
- focuses on conceptual understanding;
- provides opportunities for students to develop procedural knowledge and procedural fluency; and
- engages students in mathematical thinking.

Success Criteria

I can …
- describe an object using different measurements
- compare shapes with the same perimeter
- calculate the perimeter of a rectangle
- use the term length to describe a measurement
- use the term width to describe a measurement

Learning Goal

Students will learn to determine the lengths of a right triangle using the Pythagorean theorem.

How does this task support the role of sense maker? The task:

- has a curricular focus;
- provides opportunities for connections;
- is grounded in problem solving;
- focuses on conceptual understanding;
- provides opportunities for students to develop procedural knowledge and procedural fluency; and
- engages students in mathematical thinking.

Success Criteria

I can …
- justify why the Pythagorean theorem can be used
- explain why a second length has to be chosen before the Pythagorean theorem can be used
- determine the length of the third side using the Pythagorean theorem
- use the terms leg and hypotenuse to describe the sides of a right triangle

---

Grades 11–12: A Focus on Sense Maker

Reflect on your knowledge and understanding of graphing functions and their related reciprocal functions. Make a sketch of a primary trigonometric function and its corresponding reciprocal function.

Learning Goal

Students will learn to sketch a reciprocal trigonometric function using characteristics and strategies they used to graph function and related reciprocal functions.

How does this task support the role of sense maker? The task:

- has a curricular focus;
- provides opportunities for connections;
- provides opportunities for reflection;
- is grounded in problem solving;
- focuses on conceptual understanding; and
- engages students in mathematical thinking.

Success Criteria

I can …
- describe how zeros and/or asymptotes of functions can be used to determine characteristics of its related reciprocal function
- describe how the interval(s) on which the graph is above the x-axis can be used to determine characteristics of its related reciprocal function
- describe how the interval(s) on which the graph is below the x-axis can be used to determine characteristics of its related reciprocal function
- describe how the interval(s) on which the function is increasing can be used to determine characteristics of its related reciprocal function
- describe how the interval(s) on which the function is decreasing can be used to determine characteristics of its related reciprocal function

- describe how the point(s) where the y-value is 1and/or -1 can be used to determine characteristics of its related reciprocal function
- determine where a reciprocal trigonometric function and its corresponding primary trigonometric intersect
- determine where a reciprocal trigonometric function has a local maximum point using the local minimum point of the primary trigonometric function
- determine where a reciprocal trigonometric function has a local minimum point using the local maximum point of the primary trigonometric function
- determine the range and domain of a reciprocal trigonometric function
- describe the relationship between the characteristics of the graphs of primary trigonometric functions and their related reciprocal trigonometric functions
- make a sketch of a reciprocal trigonometric function

3   # Skill User

Over the next few weeks we focused on implementing rich tasks that support sense making to develop students' mathematical thinking. As we reflected on the notion of conceptual understanding and procedural knowledge, we realized that our beliefs and attitudes about mathematics were integral to teaching to conceptual understanding versus procedural knowledge. We were eager to further explore the concept of procedural knowledge and how it could support the role of skill user.

What is a *Skill User*?

A *skill user* recognizes and knows when and how to apply number operations, computational strategies, and procedures as a way of demonstrating procedural fluency (Fiore, Lebar, & Scott-Dunne, 2014). A skill user also uses mathematical conventions and vocabulary in oral, visual, and written form (i.e., pictorially, graphically, numerically, algebraically, or concretely) to express and organize ideas and mathematical thinking.

The Numerate Learner as a Skill User

"Students exhibit computational fluency when they demonstrate flexibility in the computational methods they choose, understand and can explain these methods, and produce accurate answers efficiently."
McClure, 2014, http://nrich.maths. org/10624

As described in Chapter 2, procedural knowledge incorporates both operational skills and basic facts and includes the knowledge of rules and procedures in mathematics and the communication of that knowledge. Procedural fluency goes one step further to include an understanding of why the procedures work. A skill implies being able to do something well or proficiently, while fluency implies having an understanding of the what, how, and why. The numerate learner demonstrates an understanding of the problem, considers possibilities, and determines when and how to take action by transferring knowledge and skills to new contexts—the numerate learner is a skill user, as described in Figure 3.1.

FIGURE 3.1: THE NUMERATE LEARNER AS A SKILL USER

A numerate learner applies ...	
Number operations	Operations include, but are not limited to: • adding • subtracting • multiplying • dividing • square root
Computations	The act of computing and calculating includes: • paper and pencil algorithm • calculator or computer • mental computation (i.e., mental math strategies) • estimation
Procedures	Methods used in computations include, but are not limited to: • arithmetic procedures (i.e., adding, subtracting, multiplying, or dividing) • simplifying • solving • factoring
Mathematical conventions	Facts or notations used in mathematics include, but are not limited to: • arrows on lines used to indicate lines are parallel • tick-marks on line segments used to indicate line segments are of equal length • order of operations
Mathematical vocabulary	Words specific to mathematics contexts can also be used in everyday language, such as: • corners on figures are called vertices • one dozen represents 12

Basic Facts: The Elephant in the Room

"Mathematics facts are important but the memorization of math facts through times table repetition, practice and timed testing is unnecessary and damaging."
Boaler, 2015, https://www.youcubed. org/fluency-without-fear/

There is no disputing that students need to know the basic facts, commonly referred to as the operations of addition, subtraction, multiplication, and division using the numbers from zero to nine. There is also no disputing that basic fact fluency is integral to the teaching and learning of mathematics and integral to the role of skill user. Basic fact fluency or automaticity is the relatively effortless recall of the basic facts. However, it is imperative that we recognize that basic fact fluency does not imply an overemphasis on rote memorization. A focus on memorizing math facts through repetition and timed testing can be damaging to how a student views mathematics and their ability to do mathematics (Boaler, 2015).

Basic Facts and Teaching and Learning in the Twenty-First Century

Having knowledge of basic facts is important and useful, but it is not sufficient when teaching for conceptual understanding and for the skills of today's teaching and learning. Although our thinking about effective teaching practices is continually evolving to adapt to environmental and societal needs, the focus of every teaching and learning experience in the classroom, regardless of the century, is driven by our students' *in the moment* needs. Teaching and learning in the twenty-first century is multi-faceted. We believe it is conducive to teaching and learning *in the moment* and therefore describe it as teaching and learning for *the now*. We need students to become skilled critical thinkers, thoughtful problem solvers, and reflective communicators—not just memorizers of basic facts.

An Opportunity for Reflection

Reflect on your perspective on what mathematics is. Does your perspective support teaching and assessing for procedural knowledge or for conceptual understanding?

What is Mathematics?

Our attitudes and beliefs about what constitutes mathematics greatly influence our teaching practices. There are varying perspectives on what mathematics is (see Figure 3.2), and those varying perspectives have the potential to influence teaching practices. Depending on our perspective of mathematics, we might emphasize or deliver different concepts in a different way (Small, 2013). For example, if we view mathematics as a set of rules and procedures and memorizing symbols and notations, then the focus in the classroom may very well be on procedural knowledge. In contrast, when we view mathematics as a way of thinking and doing, then the focus in the classroom is more likely on conceptual understanding.

FIGURE 3.2: PERSPECTIVES ON MATHEMATICS

Perspective	Description
Mathematics as a set of rules and procedures	Mathematics is viewed as a set of procedures to memorize. The focus is on the operations or procedures, such as simplifying and solving. The notion of "there is only one way to do the problem and only one answer" is often valued.
Mathematics as a hierarchy of concepts and skills	Mathematics is viewed as a hierarchical subject. The idea that there is a well-defined sequence for teaching various concepts and skills is valued (e.g., you can't teach about perimeter until you have taught length and width, or you can't teach the concept of division before you teach the concept of multiplication).
Mathematics as a study of patterns	Mathematics is distinguished from other subject areas because of its focus on patterning and its role in mathematical development.
Mathematics as a way of thinking	Mathematics is viewed in terms of the processes we use to interpret a situation. People who think mathematically see mathematics as a connected whole and use mathematics to better understand the world around them (e.g., noticing the patterns in a quilt).

Adapted from Making Math Meaningful, *Small, 2013.*

Teaching for Conceptual Understanding

Consider the following tasks.

Task A	Task B	Task C
Complete the diagram to show $\frac{1}{2} + \frac{2}{3} = \frac{7}{6}$	Add $\frac{1}{2} + \frac{2}{3}$.	Alanna thinks $\frac{1}{2} + \frac{2}{3}$ is the same as $\frac{3}{6} + \frac{4}{6}$. Austin thinks $\frac{1}{2} + \frac{2}{3}$ is the same as $\frac{6}{12} + \frac{8}{12}$. Are they both correct? Show your thinking.

Which tasks focus on conceptual understanding? Procedural knowledge? Both conceptual understanding and procedural knowledge?

Task A:
- allows for students to use a model to represent their thinking;
- does not rely on the use of rules or procedures (e.g., first check to see if the denominators are the same; if the denominators are different, make equivalent fractions using a common multiple of the two denominators; when the denominators are the same, add only the numerators and leave the denominator); and
- supports conceptual understanding.

Task B:
- supports differentiation;
- allows for students to select a strategy to represent their thinking;
- could support conceptual understanding if we encourage reasoning and proving; and
- could support procedural knowledge if we encourage the use of rules or procedures.

Task C:
- requires students to justify their thinking;
- supports reasoning and proving;
- allows students to select a strategy to represent their thinking;
- could support conceptual understanding if we encourage reasoning and proving; and
- could support procedural knowledge if we encourage the use of rules or procedures.

It is important to clarify that a task could support both conceptual understanding and procedural knowledge simultaneously. In this case, the task has the potential to support procedural fluency. When students demonstrate procedural fluency they have an understanding of why the rules or procedures work. For example, in Task C, if a student used a rule to add the fractions as part of the

"One of the gaps in many teachers' mathematical backgrounds is an internal map of the subject. They lack the fundamental understanding of how various mathematical topics interconnect, which topics are more important in the long term than others."
Small, 2009b, p. xi

solution, the teacher could further elicit the student's mathematical thinking by asking *effective questions* to confirm a conceptual understanding of why the rule works (see Figure 3.3).

FIGURE 3.3: PROCEDURAL FLUENCY

Rule Used by Student

1. To find the numerator of your final answer, multiply the numerator of each fraction by the denominator of the other fraction and then add the two numbers.

2. To find the denominator of your final answer, multiply the denominators together.

3. Simplify your answer.

Possible student response:

$$\frac{1}{2} + \frac{2}{3} = \frac{1 \times 3 + 2 \times 2}{2 \times 3}$$
$$= \frac{3 + 4}{6}$$
$$= \frac{7}{6}$$

Effective Questions Used by Teacher

- How did you show your thinking?
- How do you know the rule could be used?
- Would the rule work if you were subtracting?
- How else could you show your thinking?

Possible student response:
The rule is just a way of changing the question so that it is easier to add, like in questions where the parts are the same. I know that in order to add fractions they need to be represented by the same whole. Like denominators mean that the whole is the same. The rule can be used to think of the fractions in a different way without changing what they represent.

Procedural Fluency (an understanding of why the rule works)

An Opportunity for Reflection

A comprehensive mathematics program focuses on both procedural knowledge and conceptual understanding. How does teaching for procedural knowledge support the role of skill user? How does teaching for conceptual understanding support the role of skill user?

Using the Big Ideas of Mathematics to Support the Numerate Learner

When mathematics is viewed as a way of thinking, it is impossible for us not to refer to the big ideas in mathematics. Conversations about teaching to the important mathematical ideas, commonly referred to as the *big ideas*, are gaining ground as we shift our practices to focus on teaching for conceptual understanding. The big ideas help teachers and students make connections between new knowledge and prior learning experiences. They also link mathematical concepts between strands and other subject areas to support the development of the

"A curriculum is more than a collection of activities: it must be coherent, focused on important mathematics, and well-articulated across the grades."
NCTM, 2000, p.14

The big ideas are "fundamental principles; they are the ideas that link the specifics. Big ideas can form a framework for thinking about the important mathematics."
Small, 2009a, p. 4–5

"Some curriculum outcome/expectations are broader and more encompassing than others, but it is not obvious when you look at the curriculum. Using 'big ideas' can help teachers assess the attention or emphasis required to achieve various outcomes/expectations. Big ideas also help the teacher understand what some of the broader outcomes/expectations mean."
Small, 2009b, p. xii

numerate learner. In Chapter 1, we discussed the importance of learning goals and clearly established success criteria. The big ideas help us to define learning goals and develop success criteria that can be used to assess for learning across various strands of the curriculum.

A focus on the big ideas helps us interpret the curriculum as we plan differentiated lessons to support the needs of all learners. The big ideas link mathematical ideas into a coherent whole as we focus on developing students' mathematical thinking. A focus on the big ideas also links the four roles of the numerate learner as we concentrate on teaching for both conceptual understanding and procedural knowledge. For example, a focus on the role of skill user without focusing on sense maker isn't as meaningful, and a focus on the role of sense maker without focusing on skill user isn't as effective.

An Opportunity for Reflection

Consider the following big idea:

> *A fraction can represent parts of a region, parts of sets,*
> *parts of measures, division, or ratios.*

(Small, 2009a)

What curriculum expectations are interconnected through this big idea?

Putting it all Together

The following rich tasks support the role of skill user in effective mathematics practices and enhance students' mathematical thinking.

Grades 1–3: A Focus on Skill User

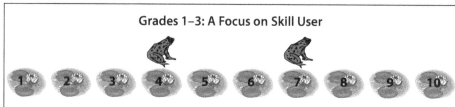

The picture shows where the frogs landed after one jump. The frogs started at 4 and 6. Create a number sentence that tells you about each frog's jump.

Adapted from Eyes on Math, *Small & Lin, 2013.*

Learning Goal

Students will learn to make generalizations related to adding zero or one that will allow them to learn two rules (i.e., adding a zero results in no change in a number, and adding one produces the next counting number) instead of individual facts.

How does this task support the role of skill user? The task:

- has a curricular focus;
- provides opportunities for connections;
- is grounded in problem solving;
- focuses on conceptual understanding;

- provides opportunities to develop procedural knowledge and procedural fluency; and
- engages students in mathematical thinking.

Success Criteria

I can …
- describe zero and explain what it means
- identify each lily pad as one
- understand that adding zero means that there is no change
- understand that adding one more means you go to the next counting number

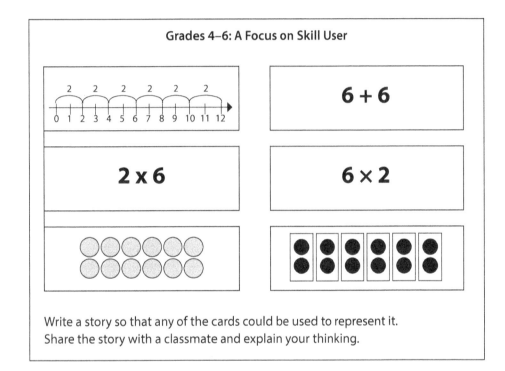

Grades 4–6: A Focus on Skill User

Write a story so that any of the cards could be used to represent it.
Share the story with a classmate and explain your thinking.

Learning Goal

Students will learn how various meanings are equivalent and how they are related to multiplication to develop automaticity.

How does this task support the role of skill user? The task:

- has a curricular focus;
- provides opportunities for connections;
- is grounded in problem solving;
- focuses on conceptual understanding;
- provides opportunities to develop procedural knowledge and procedural fluency; and
- engages students in mathematical thinking.

Success Criteria

I can …

- make connections between representations
- describe multiplication as repeated addition
- describe multiplication as equal groups
- describe multiplication as an array
- use multiplication to represent addition
- describe the meaning of addition
- describe the meaning of multiplication
- understand when to use multiplication
- understand when to use addition

Grades 7–9: A Focus on Skill User

Why does it make sense that $2(3x - 4) = 6x - 8$?

Learning Goal

Students will learn that processes that apply to operations with numbers apply to algebraic situations.

How does this task support the role of skill user? The task:

- has a curricular focus;
- provides opportunities for connections;
- is grounded in problem solving;
- focuses on conceptual understanding;
- provides opportunities to develop procedural knowledge and procedural fluency; and
- engages students in mathematical thinking.

Success Criteria

I can …

- make connections between number operations and algebraic reasoning
- describe the distributive property
- understand when to use the distributive property

Jonathan and Angelica are asked to reflect on the following question.

A quadratic equation of the form $x^2 + 8x + c$ can be factored in the form $(x + a)(x + b)$, where a and b are whole numbers.

A quadratic equation of the form $x^2 + 10x + d$ can be factored in the form $(x + e)(x + f)$, where e and f are whole numbers.

Which do you think is greater: c or d?

Jonathan thinks c is greater. Angelica thinks d is greater. Who is correct? How do you know?

Adapted from More Good Questions, *Small & Lin, 2010.*

Learning Goal

Students will learn how various procedures such as simplifying and factoring can be used to express mathematical thinking.

How does this task support the role of skill user? The task:

- has a curricular focus;
- provides opportunities for connections;
- is grounded in problem solving;
- focuses on conceptual understanding;
- provides opportunities to develop procedural knowledge and procedural fluency; and
- engages students in mathematical thinking.

Success Criteria

I can …
- make connections between simplifying and factoring
- describe when c is greater than d
- describe when d is greater than c
- describe how a and b relate
- describe how e and b relate
- describe what happens to c when a and b are close or far apart
- describe what happens to d when e and f are close or far apart
- use the distributive property to simplify the multiplication of two binomials
- factor quadratic equations

CHAPTER 4

Thought Communicator

As we continued along our learning journey, we had the opportunity to reflect on our learning with colleagues who were focusing on assessment. When considering the use of rich tasks for assessment purposes, we identified similarities in our learning. Assessing students' mathematical thinking is possible only if we implement tasks that elicit mathematical thinking and give students the opportunity to communicate their mathematical thinking. We were eager to explore the role of thought communicator, as we felt this role would help us assess for mathematical thinking as students engage in rich mathematics tasks that deepen their conceptual understanding through meaningful mathematical discussions.

What is a *Thought Communicator*?

"Communication is a critical component of learning new concepts because through articulating their understanding of a concept, students often crystallize that understanding. Mathematical communication encompasses a range of skills: reading and understanding, creating pictures and texts in a variety of formats (e.g., charts, tables, graphs, number lines), sharing ideas and discoveries through discussion, and listening to the ideas of others. Communication, combined with meaningful, guided inquiry, can help students reach their full mathematical potential."
Krpan, 2013, p. viii

A *thought communicator* communicates mathematical thinking through problem solving, reasoning, proving, reflecting, using thinking tools, connecting, and representing to gain a deeper understanding—a conceptual understanding—of mathematical concepts (Fiore, Lebar, & Scott-Dunne, 2014). A focus on communication provides opportunities for students to share ideas, respond to ideas, reflect on ideas, challenge ideas, and make connections between their thinking and the thinking of others. Students can reflect upon and make their thinking about mathematical concepts visible through communication, which includes but is not limited to communicating by:

- engaging in meaningful mathematical discussions;
- reading and writing; and
- using thinking tools.

Communicating through Meaningful Mathematical Discussions

Students are able to build upon their own thinking as well as the thinking of others through meaningful mathematical discussions. The focus on mathematical discussions to enhance students' understanding of mathematical concepts and skills is gaining ground. Although different terms are used to describe the process of communication in the context of mathematical discussions, one thing remains consistent: meaningful mathematical discussions help students to be able to make sense of the mathematics by making their thinking visible, as described in Figure 4.1.

FIGURE 4.1: TYPES OF MEANINGFUL MATHEMATICAL DISCUSSIONS

Types of Discussions	Description
Mathematical discourse	Students use mathematical discourse to make conjectures, talk, question, or agree or disagree about problems in order to discover important mathematical concepts. (Stein, 2007)
Accountable talk	"The term accountable talk refers to talk that is meaningful, respectful, and mutually beneficial to both speaker and listener. Accountable talk stimulates higher-order thinking—helping students to learn, reflect on their learning, and communicate their knowledge and understanding." (Ontario Ministry of Education, 2006)
Math talk	Teachers and students use discourse to support mathematical learning of all participants. Math talk extends one's own thinking as well as the thinking of others in the classroom. (Hufferd-Ackles, Fuson, & Sherin, 2004)
Academic conversations	Academic conversations are "exchanges between people who are trying to learn from one another and build meaning that they didn't have before. Partners take turns talking, listening, and responding to each other's comments." (Zwiers & Crawford, 2011)

The other common thread is that meaningful mathematical discussions need to be productive and adhere to students' needs. The intention is not to increase the amount of talk in the classrooms, but to increase the amount of high-quality talk (Chapin, O'Connor & Anderson, 2009). More specifically, the intent is to create learning opportunities that elicit students' mathematical thinking through purposeful and meaningful mathematical discussions. When students engage in purposeful and meaningful mathematical discussions, they:

- focus on the learning goal and established success criteria;
- respond to and build on what others have said upon reflection;
- provide evidence to support their thinking;
- question each other;
- look for connections between their thinking and the thinking of others; and
- help each other to reach a common understanding by providing convincing arguments.

Meaningful mathematical discussions present opportunities for teachers to capture students' mathematical thinking.

Although this book develops and defines four roles to support the numerate learner, connections between the four roles are inevitable. As identified in Chapter 2, effective questions provoke and develop student thinking as they engage in meaningful mathematical discussions. Purposeful and effective questions present opportunities for students to reflect on their thinking, build upon their ideas, defend their opinions, ask questions, challenge each other, draw conclusions, and make connections. Effective questions also support meaningful mathematical discussions that elicit students' mathematical thinking throughout the three-part lesson framework.

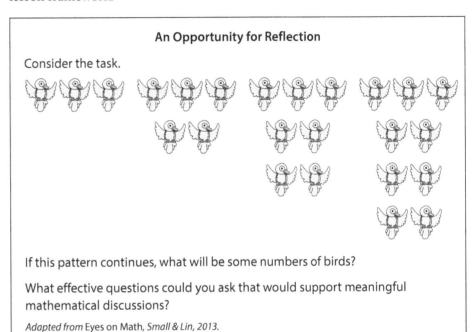

An Opportunity for Reflection

Consider the task.

If this pattern continues, what will be some numbers of birds?

What effective questions could you ask that would support meaningful mathematical discussions?

Adapted from Eyes on Math, *Small & Lin, 2013.*

Communicating through Reading and Writing

"Students who have opportunities, encouragement, and support for speaking, writing, reading, and listening in mathematics classes reap dual benefits: they communicate to learn mathematics, and they learn to communicate mathematically."
NCTM, 2000, p. 60

"Writing about mathematics encourages students to investigate concepts from a variety of perspectives, broadening their understanding of what mathematics entails. Writing also affords students time to reflect, reshape, and rework what they know."
Krpan, 2013, p. 80

Communication, whether expressed orally, visually, in writing, or through other forms of representation, is central to the teaching and learning of mathematics. As students explore, investigate, analyze, and draw conclusions, they are communicating and developing their mathematical thinking by listening, speaking, reading, and writing. When students communicate to learn mathematics through reading and writing, they are able to make sense of the mathematical concepts and skills and begin to recognize the relevance of mathematics in their everyday lives. Along with meaningful mathematics discussions, students' expression of understanding through reading and writing also provides opportunities for teachers to capture evidence of mathematical thinking in varied ways (see Figure 4.2).

FIGURE 4.2: EVIDENCE OF MATHEMATICAL THINKING IN READING AND WRITING

Reading in Mathematics	Writing in Mathematics
• Students can analyze, evaluate, interpret, recognize biases, and understand a variety of texts from different mathematical contexts, such as the media, picture books, magazines, and written and graphic information presented in math tasks. • Students can apply the information they have read for different purposes.	• Students can communicate their ideas using a variety of writing formats such as tables, diagrams, charts, graphs, and number lines. • Students can classify their ideas by using graphic and written representations, such as number lines, tallies, lists, notes, highlighting, and/or underlining key words/ phrases.
• Students can make connections between math texts and their personal lives. • Students can make connections between math texts and other subject areas. • Students can make connections between math texts and various topics of mathematics. • Students can make connections between different math texts and identify similarities and differences between them. • Students are able to interpret and decode the meaning of mathematics symbols, conventions, models, and pictures. • Students are able to apply a variety of strategies (e.g., visualize, infer, predict, ask questions, re-read) to help them understand the mathematics they read.	• Students can organize their ideas in a variety of ways such as using graphic organizers like a Venn diagram to compare and contrast information, a T-chart to support problem solving, and electronic-based tools to create spreadsheets and concept maps. • Students can gather information to help determine importance, such as scan math texts for key information and locate and identify key words/ ideas. • Students use appropriate mathematical vocabulary and conventions. • Students use pictures, numbers, or words to show their understanding of mathematical concepts and skills. • Students provide examples to support their mathematical thinking using written and graphic information. • Students can revise their writing based on feedback from peers and/ or teachers. • Students can make connections to real-world situations.

Adapted from Math Expression, *Krpan, 2013 and* The Ontario Curriculum Grades 1–8: Language, *Ontario Ministry of Education, 2006.*

Communicating through the Use of Thinking Tools

When used purposefully, thinking tools, such as manipulatives and technology, allow us to make sense of concepts. Thinking tools can include physical or virtual objects that can be physically manipulated to demonstrate, model, and communicate mathematical thinking. Students deepen their conceptual understanding of mathematical concepts when they use thinking tools to represent their thinking or the thinking of others. They provide an opportunity for students to make connections between various representations and build knowledge by exploring, creating, and discovering.

Fractions, or more specifically equivalent fractions, provide an example of how thinking tools can be used to enhance mathematical thinking. If a fraction represents a number, an equivalent fraction is simply another name for the same amount (Small, 2014). Equivalent fractions in particular illustrate the power of how thinking tools can be used to deepen students' conceptual understanding. The following statement or rule may resonate with some: *To find an equivalent fraction, multiply or divide the numerator and the denominator by the same number.* It is no surprise that many students and even some adults struggle with fractions. The teaching of fractions and operations with fractions often incorporates the use of rules such as the one noted above. It is evident in this case that the focus is on rules and procedures, and mathematics is viewed as such. However, when mathematics is seen as a way of thinking and the focus is on conceptual understanding for the purpose of sense making, students explore equivalent fractions by using various thinking tools.

Consider the following task.

State another fraction that means the same as $\frac{2}{3}$.

Now consider the possible solutions.

Solution A

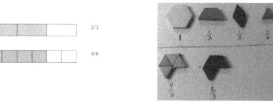

$$\frac{2}{3} = \frac{8}{12}$$

Solution B

▭ 2/3	
▭ 4/6	

Solution C

Solution D

Solution A:
- uses the rule of "multiply the numerator and denominator by the same number" to find an equivalent fraction;
- confirms procedural knowledge;
- does not confirm conceptual understanding; and
- does not confirm procedural fluency.

Solutions B–D:
- use thinking tools; and
- confirm conceptual understanding.

Thinking tools allow students to construct their own meaning as opposed to relying on a set of rules or procedures. It is important to clarify that thinking tools can be any physical objects. Pattern blocks and fraction strips, along with buttons, bottle caps, and dried beans all have the potential to enhance students' mathematical thinking when used purposefully.

An Opportunity for Reflection

What questions could you ask to ensure that the student who provided Solution A (in the previous example) had a conceptual understanding of equivalent fractions?

Use another thinking tool to find an equivalent fraction of $\frac{2}{3}$.

The Role of Mathematical Content Knowledge for Teaching: The Other Elephant in the Room

"Knowing mathematics for teaching demands a kind of depth well beyond what is needed to carry out the algorithm reliably."
Ball, Hill, & Bass, 2005, p. 22

Many myths are associated with the teaching and learning of mathematics. We like to think of them as the elephants in the room that, at times, surface and result in very difficult conversations, and at other times are often neglected. We addressed one of the elephants in the room in Chapter 3: basic facts. However, there is another elephant—*content knowledge for teaching*—that is equally as challenging. Some myths about content knowledge for teaching include the following:

- You have to have a math brain to do well in mathematics.
- You have to have a mathematics background to effectively teach mathematics.
- Boys are better at mathematics than girls.
- Problem solving is all about word problems.
- You have to have the basic facts memorized before you can engage in problem solving.

"Although many studies demonstrate that teachers' mathematical knowledge helps support increased student achievement, that actual nature and extent of that knowledge—whether it is simply basic skills at the grades they teach, or complex and professional specific mathematical knowledge—is largely unknown."
Ball, Hill, & Bass, 2005, p. 16

Mathematical content knowledge for teaching refers to a kind of professional knowledge of mathematics that is tailored to the work teachers do with the curriculum and students. It differs from mathematical knowledge such as knowledge of advanced calculus and differential equations (Ball, Hill & Bass, 2005). Simply stated, teachers need to have mathematical content knowledge for teaching that will enhance their students' understanding of mathematical concepts. Referring back to our example using fractions, if we want students to have a deep conceptual understanding of equivalent fractions and we want students to think differently about equivalent fractions, then we need to teach fractions differently. To teach fractions differently, we need to develop our mathematical content knowledge of fractions for teaching so we can effectively implement teaching practices to enhance our students' understanding of fractions. Knowledge of advanced calculus and differential calculus won't necessarily help. Having mathematical content knowledge for teaching helps us purposefully select and use rich mathematics tasks that support conceptual understanding and sense making, develop students' mathematical thinking, anticipate student responses and possible misconceptions, and develop and incorporate effective questions to provide opportunities for students to communicate their thinking.

Putting it all Together

The following rich tasks support the role of thought communicator through effective mathematics practices and enhance students' mathematical thinking.

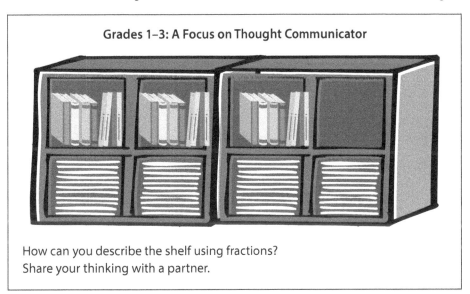

Grades 1–3: A Focus on Thought Communicator

How can you describe the shelf using fractions?
Share your thinking with a partner.

Learning Goal

Students will learn to describe a fraction as being part of a set.

How does this task support the role of thought communicator? The task:

- has a curricular focus;
- provides opportunities for students to share their thinking;
- provides opportunities for students to compare their thinking with others;
- is grounded in problem solving;
- focuses on conceptual understanding;
- engages students in mathematical thinking; and
- engages students in meaningful mathematical discussions.

Success Criteria

I can …
- understand that the whole has 8 equal parts
- identify each shelf as $\frac{1}{8}$ of the whole
- understand that $\frac{4}{8}$ is the same as $\frac{1}{2}$
- describe how the books make up $\frac{3}{8}$ of the shelf
- describe how the baskets take up $\frac{4}{8}$ of the shelf

---

Grades 6–8: A Focus on Thought Communicator

Write a word problem to match the equation.

$$250 = 20n + 150$$

Share the word problem with a classmate and explain your thinking.

Learning Goal

Students will learn how to translate algebraic expressions into statements describing mathematical relationships.

How does this task support the role of thought communicator? The task:

- has a curricular focus;
- provides opportunities for students to share their thinking;
- provides opportunities for students to compare their thinking with others;
- is grounded in problem solving;
- focuses on conceptual understanding;
- offers opportunities to develop procedural knowledge and procedural fluency;
- engages students in mathematical thinking; and
- engages students in meaningful mathematical discussions.

Success Criteria

I can …
- make connections between statements
- connect contextual situations with equations

- describe how my word problem uses the coefficient of n
- describe what the variable, n, is in the word problem
- describe how I use the constant, 150, in the word problem
- describe what led me to the word problem I created

Grades 7–10: A Focus on Thought Communicator

The length of one leg of a right triangle is 20 cm. What does that tell you about the other sides? The angles? Share your thinking with a classmate.

Learning Goal

Student will learn to describe how knowing a measurement of a right triangle can help you determine other measurements of the same right triangle.

How does this task support the role of thought communicator? The task:

- has a curricular focus;
- provides opportunities for students to share their thinking;
- provides opportunities for students to compare their thinking with others;
- provides opportunities for students to reflect on their thinking;
- is grounded in problem solving;
- focuses on conceptual understanding;
- engages students in mathematical thinking; and
- engages students in meaningful mathematical discussions.

Success Criteria

I can …
- explain how the Pythagorean theorem can be used to find the lengths of the other sides given the measurement of one leg
- explain how the primary trigonometric ratios can be used to find the measures of the angles of a right triangle
- explain the relationship between the sides of a right triangle and the Pythagorean theorem
- explain the relationship between the sides and angles of a right triangle and the primary trigonometric ratios
- explain why a second length has to be chosen before the Pythagorean theorem can be used to find the lengths
- explain how the measures of the angles in a right triangle can be determined using the primary trigonometric ratios
- explain how the length of the third side can be determined using the Pythagorean theorem or a primary trigonometric ratio
- use the terms leg and hypotenuse to describe the sides of a right triangle

How is a quadratic function the same as its reciprocal function? How are they different?

Graph a quadratic function and its reciprocal.

Learning Goal

Students will learn to explain how the key characteristics of a quadratic function can be used to graph its related reciprocal function.

How does this task support the role of thought communicator? The task:

- has a curricular focus;
- provides opportunities for students to share their thinking;
- provides opportunities for students to reflect;
- provides opportunities for students to compare their thinking with others;
- is grounded in problem solving;
- focuses on conceptual understanding;
- engages students in mathematical thinking; and
- engages students in meaningful mathematical discussions.

Success Criteria

I can …

- explain why the y-coordinates of a reciprocal function are the reciprocals of the original function
- identify the vertical asymptotes of the reciprocal function based on the zeros of the original function
- determine the horizontal asymptote of the reciprocal function
- explain why a reciprocal function has the same positive intervals as the original function
- explain why a reciprocal function has the same negative intervals as the original function
- explain why the intervals of increase on the original function are the intervals of decrease on the related reciprocal function
- explain why the intervals of decrease on the original function are the intervals of increase on the related reciprocal function
- explain why if the original function has a local minimum point, the reciprocal function will have a local maximum point at the same x-value
- explain why if the original function has a local maximum point, the reciprocal function will have a local minimum point at the same x-value
- explain that the reciprocal function will intersect the original function at the point or points where the y-coordinate is 1 or –1 if the range of the original function includes 1 and/or –1
- make a sketch of a quadratic and its reciprocal function using the characteristics noted above

5 Critical Interpreter

As you deepen your understanding of sense maker, skill user, and thought communicator, you will recognize that these three roles are integrated and interconnected in supporting the development of the numerate learner. But the question still remains: How can you create learning experiences that engage students in critical thought about using mathematics to respond to a situation and possibly transform it? It is particularly intriguing to explore the role of critical interpreter through the lens of mathematics. Students can use critical thinking skills in mathematics to challenge the status quo and disrupt commonly held assumptions about issues, events, and situations in their everyday world. The role of critical interpreter will help students better understand the connections between mathematics and numeracy.

What is a *Critical Interpreter*?

A *critical interpreter* applies mathematical knowledge and skills beyond the mathematics classroom to challenge power and bias in mathematical ideas and thinking. This might include the use of numbers, patterns, measurements, graphs, shapes, figures, pictures, and/or statistics. Using a critical numeracy lens, a critical interpreter examines the role mathematics plays in the world in relation to political and moral issues. Thinking is central to learning mathematics as students engage in tasks that provide them with opportunities to make sense of mathematical concepts. Thinking critically is an important facet of the teaching and learning process in the context of twenty-first century learning, and central to being a critical interpreter. By seeing critical numeracy as a lens for learning, students are empowered to use numeracy to support their biases, perspectives, and ideas (Fiore, Lebar, & Scott-Dunne, 2014).

The role of critical interpreter adds a dimension to the teaching and learning of mathematics that helps deepen students' understanding of how mathematics can be used to potentially transform the world. Promoting this critical numeracy lens is integral to developing active citizens who participate responsibly and morally in a democratic society. Students need to be able to view the world around them from different perspectives so they can recognize unjust situations and take action to promote fairness and equity.

Consider the graphs in Figure 5.1.

FIGURE 5.1: SAMPLE GRAPHS

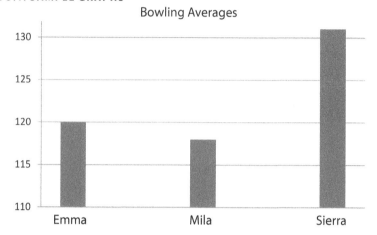

Graph 1

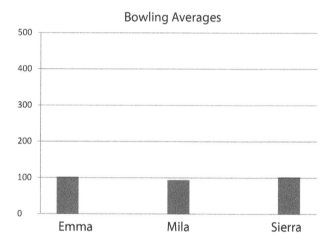

Graph 2

At first glance, Graph 1 seems to show that Sierra has a substantially higher score than Emma and Mila. However, upon further reflection and critical thinking, it becomes evident that Graph 1 is not fairly represented. Although the y-axis increases by increments of five, it does not start at zero. The y-axis has not been properly subdivided and does not begin at the origin. When the graph is fairly represented, as in Graph 2, it is evident that Sierra's score is in fact not much higher than the other scores.

As students make sense of relationships and representing them graphically, they can then begin to use this knowledge and understanding to critically interpret information presented in visual representations. In this case, students require a deep understanding of how graphs can be properly used to represent relationships in order to identify the misrepresentation.

Understanding Critical Literacy

To better understand the role of critical interpreter in mathematics, it is important to review and reflect on the principles of critical literacy. According to Paulo Freire (1970), critical literacy focuses on issues of power and promotes reflection, transformation, and action. Freire developed the notion of *praxis*, which requires people to reflect on their social, economic, and political realities, and to act on the knowledge acquired to transform these current realities by making changes in their local and global communities (Freire, 1970).

Freire also challenged the dehumanizing banking approach to education, which viewed learners as empty bank accounts that need to be deposited with knowledge. He disrupted this way of thinking about teaching and learning by introducing a problem-posing approach that moved learners from being passive in the learning process to being active participants. Being critically literate is, therefore, about learning to read the world and engaging in practices that encourage learners to question and challenge the beliefs and value messages expressed by authors.

Being critically aware helps learners develop a critical stance to identify and interrogate ideologies, identities, and values that are presented in a variety of social, economic, or political contexts. Building critical awareness is connected to an individual's literacy identity, which is shaped by the person's social and cultural experiences (Anstey & Bull, 2006). This is why educators often think of ways to activate students' prior knowledge before introducing a new concept and/or skill. Students' social or cultural experiences may influence the way they think about an idea, read and interpret a text, or even execute a task (Anstey & Bull, 2006). Being critically literate is about interacting with knowledge and ideas in a reflective and active manner, as opposed to passively receiving and accepting information without questioning authority, purpose, authenticity, reliability, relevancy, and accuracy.

This notion of critical literacy certainly supports the idea that readers should not believe everything they read and that there is always another perspective that is missing. Texts are created with an intended purpose by an author who makes intentional choices about audience, style, format, language, text features, and the use of literacy devices to convey value-laden messages about a topic, issue, or concept. The ideas expressed are therefore biased, and perhaps only shared from one perspective.

In Luke and Freebody's *Four Roles of the Literate Learner* framework (1990), the role of "text analyzer" is intended to help readers examine the critical analysis process when using texts. Anstey and Bull (2006) affirm, indicating that being a proficient text analyst involves understanding how texts affect our view of the world and how they shape our behaviour and lives. It is, therefore, critical to engage students in focused conversations about texts that will help foster a mindset of transformation leading to action. We can ask questions to encourage discussions about critically examining the purpose of texts, as shown in Figure 5.2.

"Critical literacy helps us move beyond that passive acceptance and take an active role in the reader-author relationship by questioning issues such as who wrote the text, what the author wanted us to believe, and what information the author chose to include or exclude in the text."
McLaughlin & DeVoogd, 2004, p. 6

"We need critical literacy because it helps us: (1) to establish equal status in the reader-author relationship; (2) to understand the motivation the author had for writing the text (function) and how the author uses the text to make us understand in a particular way (form); (3) to understand that the author's perspective is not the only perspective; and (4) to become active users of the information in texts to develop independent perspectives, as opposed to being passive reproducers of the ideas in texts."
McLaughlin & DeVoogd, 2004, p. 7

Theory into Practice

Questions about the LITERACY LEARNING TASKS:

- What is the purpose of this literacy learning task? What is the learning goal for this task?
- Who is involved with this literacy learning task and with what interests and values?
- Why am I involved—what are my purposes, interests, and values?
- Is there social and cultural knowledge or experience that will help me in this situation?

Questions about the TEXTS:

- What is the purpose of this text? What is it trying to achieve?
- How does the purpose of this text shape the genre, form, structure, organizational pattern, use of language, and/or word choice? What can I expect to encounter?
- What do I know about this genre and texts that will help me identify dominant positions and beliefs?
- What do I know about this genre and texts that will help me identify beliefs and positions that are being silenced?
- What is the origin of this text? Who is the author? What authority does the author have?
- How does the origin of this text affect the way in which I should position myself when I read it?

Questions about the TRANSFORMATION:

- What is my desired relationship with the participants involved with this literacy learning task, and how will I behave?
- How will this affect my use of language (e.g., choice of vocabulary)?
- What do I think about this text and the implied ideas/messages?
- What is the text trying to make me believe, think, or do?
- Whose voice is represented in this text? Whose voice is missing?
- Who is being advantaged? Who is being marginalized?
- What alternatives are there to the beliefs and ideas presented in this text?
- How might I reconstruct or modify this text as I use it for this learning task?
- What actions will I take as a result of my text analysis?

Teaching and Learning Multiliteracies, *Anstey & Bull, 2006, p. 52.*

If students are going to be actively involved in creating change in their local and/ or global communities, then they must develop a repertoire of literate practices that include the dimension of critical analysis. These practices will require them to question the status quo, consider alternative perspectives, and take actions that will positively affect their social, economic, and political futures.

Connecting Critical Literacy to Critical Numeracy

"Critical numeracy sets out to encourage students to see that mathematical practice is always morally and politically loaded—and that when mathematics is used in practical situations, students should understand and reflect on the world position of those using it."
Stoessiger, 2002, p. 48

If literacy can be used to make the world a better place, can numeracy be used in the same way to change the way we view the world? Numeracy can support and enhance how we function and participate actively in society. Calculating discounts when shopping, measuring and estimating when cooking, calculating tips and taxes at restaurants, creating budget plans based on earnings and expenses, and banking and managing finances (including investing, saving, exploring mortgage rates, and understanding interest rates) are just a few examples of how numeracy applies to real-world contexts. But how do mathematical knowledge and skills foster a critical mindset? How might this be possible, and what are the implications for the teaching and learning of mathematics? How can the dimensions of critical literacy be applied to support critical numeracy?

By reflecting on the characteristics of critical literacy, we can conclude that the ideas that shape the notion of being critically literate can be used to build an understanding of what it means to be critically numerate. After all, adopting a critical stance is an attitude—a way of thinking and being—that allows students to actively and consciously participate in the learning process. This would mean that using a critical analysis approach to teaching and learning is cross-curricular and interdisciplinary, as described in Chapter 1. Figure 5.3 shows how to begin unpacking the dimensions of critical numeracy.

FIGURE 5.3: THE DIMENSIONS OF CRITICAL NUMERACY

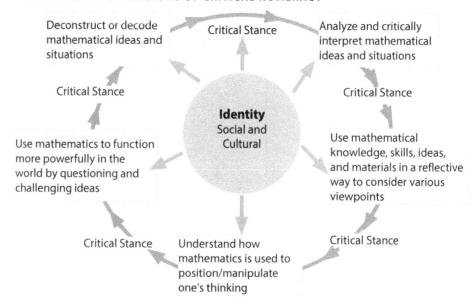

First, it is important to clarify that like the texts used to develop literacy skills, mathematical ideas carry value messages. This means they are not neutral and bias free. The user of a particular mathematical idea is attempting to manipulate another user to think in a similar manner. For example, if we closely examine the two advertisements below, we might consider the following reflective questions:

- What assumptions can be made?
- Who are the creators?
- What is the intended purpose?
- What role do mathematical knowledge and skills play?
- What role do language and literacy play?
- How are the advertisements trying to position the consumer?
- How will the advertisements be interpreted?
- Who will benefit from these advertisements?

It is clear that the advertisers' ultimate goal is to increase sales and increase revenue. They have created value-laden advertisements with the intent of convincing consumers that they are getting a deal. The advertisers have used various persuasive techniques and, therefore, consumers need to deconstruct and make sense of them to determine how they are being manipulated.

To decode, analyze, and interpret the advertisements, consumers must consider the language used and understand specific mathematical concepts. For example, they need to understand what "BOGO" and "Buy One Get One ½ Off" mean. They also need to understand fractions, ratios, percents, and the relationship between them. What does ½ mean? What does 50% off mean? Consumers can then use their language and mathematical knowledge to critically interpret the advertisements and reflect on how they can question the messaging. Are the advertisements actually conveying two different messages, or is the underlying message in each one the same?

An Opportunity for Reflection

Which could be considered the better deal—a product that is 25% off the regular price, or the same product that is selling at regular price but has 25% more quantity? Justify your thinking.

"Critical numeracy encompasses the many ways by which students learn not only to use or access mathematics in the world but at the same time investigate the social practices involved, reflect on the effects on power relationships and seek to understand their consequences for themselves and others."
Stoessiger, 2002, p. 50

For example, the picture book *The Waterhole* by Graeme Base (2001) engages students in a discussion about transformation and taking action to support a sustainable future for Earth. The story demonstrates the impact that diminishing natural resources, like water, have on the environment and its various habitats. The "waterhole" represents the world's water supply and what happens when it dries out. It emphasizes the importance of water to all living things. Clearly, the book addresses the concept of counting and requires an understanding of mathematics. An understanding of volume, capacity, and ratio would help students to make connections and predictions (e.g., How much rain is needed to fill the waterhole? How many rain droplets can sustain the life of animals?).

Being critically numerate also includes reflecting on how students can use their cultural and social experiences to support their critical mathematical thinking about ecosystems and actions that they can take to help with the future sustainability of their planet. The concept of drought and/or saving water may be very different for some students depending on where they have lived. For example, students who have lived only in North America may interpret drought as having no rain for three weeks in the summer, while for students who have lived in Africa, Asia, or Australia, the reality of drought is no rain for a very long period of time. These multiple viewpoints would most likely emerge from critical reflection of the story and meaningful mathematics discussions, as students use their mathematics knowledge of various concepts like counting, volume, capacity, and ratio to make interpretations and plan collective actions to protect the future of their environment from shortage of water and depletion of other natural resources.

A number of characteristics of critical numeracy have real-world implications (Kerka, 1995). For example, critical numeracy:

- is culturally-based and socially constructed;
- reflects cultural values;
- is not just about numbers;
- considers multiple viewpoints about mathematical situations and ideas;
- disrupts commonly held assumptions about numbers, measurements, patterns, graphs, statistics, and other mathematical concepts/ideas;
- is about using mathematics to create fairness in the world; and
- recognizes that mathematical ideas are not neutral.

Consider the following task.

The unemployment rate can be defined as the number of people unemployed divided by the number of people in the labour force.

 Consider the following figures from Ontario:

1.   5,500,000 people are employed full-time
2.   1,000,000 people are employed part-time and want part-time work
3.   220,000 people are employed part-time and want full-time work
4.   300,000 are not employed, looked for work in the last month, and are not on temporary layoff
5.   60,000 are not employed and are on a temporary layoff
6.   22,000 are not employed, want a job now, looked for work in the last year, or stopped looking for work because they were discouraged about the possibility of finding work
7.   76,000 are not employed, want a job now, looked for work in the last year, or stopped looking for work for other reasons
8.   3,300,000 are not employed and don't want a job now

Calculate the unemployment rate in Ontario.

Adapted from Rethinking Mathematics: Teaching Social Justice by the Numbers, *Gutstein & Peterson, 2006.*

If we deconstruct this task through the lens of the characteristics of critical numeracy, the task requires an understanding of mathematics, but it also involves political struggle: How do we decide who makes up the "number of unemployed" and the "total labour force"? It is this political struggle that supports critical numeracy. Figure 5.4 outlines possible questions to ask to encourage critical thinking.

FIGURE 5.4: QUESTIONS TO ENCOURAGE CRITICAL NUMERACY

Theory into Practice

- For whom are these ideas intended?
- For whom have these questions and problems been developed?
- Who is doing the math?
- Who would benefit from these mathematical ideas?
- What is missing?
- Whose voice is not represented?
- Is the mathematical thinking represented fairly?
- Are there viewpoints that have not been considered?
- What is the bias in the representation of the data?

"Students can be empowered as creators of mathematics for their own purposes. They are able to select numbers, measurements or shapes to support their arguments and are aware of how to use them effectively in particular social contexts. They are competent and creative in the use of mathematical information as ways of illustrating ideas or enlisting support for their viewpoint."
Stoessiger, 2002, p. 51

Critical numeracy is about empowerment and how mathematics is used in the world (Stoessiger, 2002). What are the implications of teaching to ensure students are empowered to learn mathematics to become more critically numerate? Students must see the importance and relevancy in the mathematics that they learn and do. They need to view mathematics as a way of thinking and as a way of making the world a better place. To foster empowerment, educators can help students develop an understanding that mathematical ideas aim to position them in certain ways (Stoessiger, 2002). To combat this intentional manipulation, students need to learn how to critique this positioning by questioning and challenging the mathematical ideas, questions, and problem-solving tasks presented in a particular manner.

Half of the grain grown around the world is fed to livestock, while one billion people around the world do not get enough to eat. If cattle were able to graze freely in pastures, their meat would be leaner and healthier. Instead, most cattle today are penned up in crowded "feedlots" and fed large quantities of grain. Cows need to eat 14 kilograms of grain and drink 18,000 litres of water to give us only 1 kilogram of meat to eat. Many people around the world do not have access to clean water and must walk long distances every day to get it. Only people with enough money can afford to eat meat on a regular basis.

If everyone in your class ate a 115 g burger, how much grain and water was used to produce the class's lunch? Do you think this is a problem? If it is a problem, what are some possible solutions?

How might this problem support the role of critical interpreter?

Adapted from Rethinking Mathematics: Teaching Social Justice by the Numbers, *Gutstein & Peterson, 2006.*

Using Critical Social Practice to Develop a Critical Stance

Critical numeracy, like critical literacy, is about empowerment, freedom, and hope. These are fostered by adopting a critical stance, which is an attitude and a way of thinking and acting. Lewison, Leland, and Harste (2008) expand on the four dimensions of critical social practice originally developed by Lewison, Flint, and Van Sluys (2002). They are "disrupting the commonplace, interrogating multiple viewpoints, focusing on socio-political issues, and taking action to promote social justice" (p. xxv).

Figure 5.5 begins to deconstruct each dimension through several thought-provoking questions to support critical reflection.

Using Social Practices to Develop a CRITICAL STANCE	
Disrupt the commonplace?	**Consider multiple viewpoints?**
Disrupt stereotypes and commonly held assumptions What does the author want us to believe? What assumptions is the author making about us as readers?	**Understanding Texts on Different Levels** I wonder how this story might have been different if it had been written by someone of the opposite gender, different religion, or different ethnic group.
How can we use mathematics to uncover stereotypes? How can math concepts such as percentages, proportions and comparisons be used to help students question and discuss the information that they have uncovered? How can implementing "mathematics across the curriculum" better help students ask questions and clarify social issues?	**Connecting Mathematics to Students' Lives?** How can students explore the use of math in their homes and communities? How can the use of numbers and math in news articles, literature, and everyday events help students realize that math is more than computation and definitions?
Focus on the socio-political?	**Take action to promote social justice?**
Understanding social and/or political issues between individuals or in society at large What are the economic issues that underlie this text? What are some parts of this text that really bother you politically? How else might these have been written? How can **mathematics** be used to deepen students' understanding of important social and global issues?	**Understanding ways in which people can be powerful in their own words** What could we do that would call attention to issues both in school and out of school? How can students understand their own power as active citizens in building a democratic society and play a more active role in that society?

Adapted from Creating Critical Classrooms – K–8 Reading and Writing with an Edge, *Lewison, Leland & Harste (2008) and* Rethinking Mathematics: Teaching Social Justice by the Numbers, *Gutstein & Peterson (2006).*

This framework supports a reflexive and responsive mindset where we are always questioning the status quo. Teachers and students can use the dimensions of critical social practice to help them adopt a critical stance so they can view the world from multiple perspectives and decide how they might thoughtfully respond to various situations. It is important to always begin with getting to know the students' interests, knowledge, and social and cultural experiences so that we can build on these resources and use the questioning that supports the dimensions of critical social practice to inquire, interrogate, and investigate the everyday world (Lewison, Leland, & Harste, 2008).

Figure 5.6 uses the unemployment problem presented earlier (see page 70) as an example of using the framework to help foster a critical stance.

Disrupt the Commonplace	Consider Multiple Viewpoints
Consider the beliefs and assumptions associated with "unemployment" and the "labour force." • What does "unemployment" mean? • How is "labour force" defined? • Who makes up the "number of unemployed" and the "total labour force"? • Are the data represented fairly? • Is there anything missing? • Who is doing the math?	The data represented is for Ontario only. • How might our understanding of "unemployment" and the "labour force" change if data from other provinces and/or countries are examined? • Who is presenting this data? Is it Statistics Canada? • Was a particular labour force survey used? • Whose voice is not represented? • Do the data presented consider demographics and regions of Ontario? How can students' understanding of proportional reasoning help solve the problem from multiple and contradictory viewpoints?
Focus on the Socio-Political	**Take Action to Promote Social Justice**
We need to understand and question the political and social structures that create conditions of unemployment. Investigating relationships of power and language used to maintain domination would help us understand the complexities surrounding "unemployment" (Lewison, Leland, & Harste, 2008). For example, *22,000 not employed, want a job now, looked for work in the last year, stopped looking because discouraged about prospects of finding work.* • Why is this group discouraged? • Is this group being marginalized as a result of diversity, access, or lanuage? How can students use their understanding of the relationships involving percent, ratio, and unit rate to help them understand the political structures surrounding "unemployment"?	Through reflection and critical thought that emerge from using the other social practices, we might recognize a need to take action to transform a situation. Action can often take different forms, such as having an awareness, taking responsibility to inquire, being reflexive, entertaining alternate ways of being, and consciously engaging (Lewison, Leland & Harste, 2008). With respect to the unemployment problem, students may decide to conduct a "labour force" survey in their community to gather data that actually pertain to their local community. They may choose to write a letter to Statistics Canada asking to clarify the data presented so that all viewpoints are considered (e.g., demographics, regions).

Putting it all Together

Grades 1–3: A Focus on Critical Interpreter

Have students draw pictures or make models that represent different professions (e.g., police officer, accountant) and roles (e.g., stay-home parent, caregiver). Collect individual drawings and models. As a whole class, sort/group drawings and models according to gender.

Use the data to discuss how gender, societal, and/or cultural difference impact professions and roles.

Learning Goal

Students will learn to use, collect, and interpret data.

How does this task support the role of critical interpreter? The task:

- has a curricular focus;
- provides opportunities for students to share their thinking;
- challenges the use of mathematics to identify biases and perceptions;
- engages students in mathematical thinking;
- offers opportunities for students to compare their thinking with others; and
- engages students in meaningful mathematical discussions.

Success Criteria

I can …

- sort pictures and models using characteristics
- draw conclusions based on the data and explain my thinking
- identify how my personal experiences impact my thinking

Grades 6–8: A Focus on Critical Interpreter

A department store is offering an additional 40% off for only one day. Austin and Alanna see a shirt for $50 that is in a clearance section. All the items in the clearance section are 30% off. Alanna decides to buy the shirt and she is very excited because she thinks she will get a 70% discount. Austin disagrees and claims the total discount will be less than 70%. At the checkout, the sales attendant takes 30% of the original price and then takes an additional 40% off the sales price.

Who was right? Explain your thinking.

30% off; Regular price $50

Today Only!
Take an
Additional
40% off

Adapted from ONAP 8, Small, 2010.

Learning Goal

Students will learn that the amount a percent represents is based on the whole of which it is a percent.

How does this task support the role of critical interpreter? The task:

- has a curricular focus;
- engages students in mathematical thinking;
- provides opportunities for students to share their thinking;
- challenges the use of percents;
- provides opportunities to understand the motivation behind the advertisement;
- offers opportunities for students to compare their thinking with others;
- is grounded in problem solving;
- focuses on conceptual understanding; and
- engages students in meaningful mathematical discussions.

Success Criteria

I can …
- understand that percents are a ratio where the second term is 100
- identify that I have to calculate 30% of the original price
- identify that I have to calculate 40% of the sale price
- understand that the entire discount is not 70% of the original price
- provide an explanation for my reasoning

Grades 7–9: A Focus on Critical Interpreter

Consider the following.

CEO to Worker Pay Ratio 1978–2013

What information does this graph show you? What do you wonder about the information presented in the graph? What question would you ask to support your sense of wonder? Share the question with a classmate.

Learning Goal

Students will learn to read, interpret, make inferences, and pose questions from a graphical display.

How does this task support the role of critical interpreter? The task:

- has a curricular focus;
- provides opportunities for students to share their thinking;
- challenges the use of mathematics to identify biases and perceptions;
- engages students in mathematical thinking;
- offers opportunities for students to compare their thinking with others; and
- engages students in meaningful mathematical discussions.

Success Criteria

I can ...

- make interpretations based on the data
- draw conclusions based on the data and explain my thinking
- identify how my personal experiences impact my thinking
- pose questions based on my interpretations

Grades 9–12: A Focus on Critical Interpreter

The graph shows the percentage of adult Internet users who use social networking sites by gender.

Analyze the data. Using the information presented and not represented, state a conclusion. Explain your reasoning. What do you predict the trends to be in 10 years?

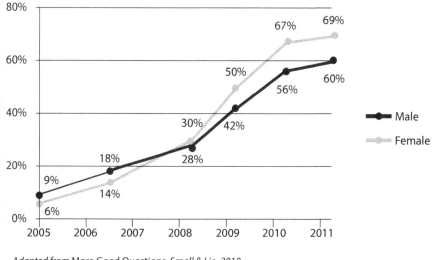

Social Networking Site Use by Gender, 2005–2011

Adapted from More Good Questions, *Small & Lin, 2010.*

Learning Goal

Students will learn to read, interpret, make inferences, and pose questions from a graphical display.

How does this task support the role of critical interpreter? The task:

- has a curricular focus;
- provides opportunities for students to share their thinking;
- challenges the use of mathematics to identify biases and perceptions;
- engages students in mathematical thinking;
- offers opportunities for students to compare their thinking with others; and
- engages students in meaningful mathematical discussions.

Success Criteria

I can …
- make interpretations based on the data
- identify trends and justify my thinking
- identify how my personal experiences impact my thinking
- pose questions based on my interpretations
- make predictions based on the information presented and explain why they make sense

CHAPTER 6

Moving Forward

We began our exploration of teaching mathematics today by developing a framework, the *Four Roles of the Numerate Learner*. We explored the four roles and reflected on how we could use each role to support student learning and thinking. We considered our beliefs about the teaching and learning of mathematics and examined instructional and assessment strategies that enhance student understanding of mathematical concepts. As we continue with our personal inquiries, this chapter consolidates our thinking and learning so that we can embrace the *Four Roles of the Numerate Learner* framework to support interdisciplinary thinking in the context of twenty-first century teaching and learning.

Where Do We Go from Here?

Although our thinking about effective teaching practices is continually evolving to adapt to environmental and societal needs, the focus of every teaching and learning experience in the classroom, regardless of the century, is driven by our students' *in the moment* needs. Teaching and learning today is conducive to teaching and learning for *the now* or *in the moment*. Teaching and learning for *the now* means that we are focusing on our students' *in the moment* needs, rather than what worked 15 years ago or what will work 15 years from now. To do this, we need responsive and adaptive teaching practices that promote critical thinking and reflective communication.

Through the lens of literacy, this means reflecting on how the *Four Roles of the Literate Learner* framework supports teaching and learning for *the now*. Through the lens of numeracy, it means reflecting on how the *Four Roles of the Numerate Learner* framework supports teaching and learning for *the now*. Through the lens of teaching and learning, it simply means reflecting on students' *in the moment* needs and intentionally responding to those needs to support the skills of collaboration, critical thinking, problem solving, creativity, and communicating. Keep in mind that reflecting and knowing are necessary but not sufficient if we are going to alter the way students view mathematics. It is the doing—the responding—that is crucial!

Whether we are referring to the *Four Roles of the Literate Learner* or the *Four Roles of the Numerate Learner*, it is important to acknowledge that these frameworks are simply a way of thinking. The focus is on thinking differently about the way we view the curriculum content and doing things differently to support the development of skills necessary to function in today's world. The *Four Roles of the Numerate Learner* framework not only values interdisciplinary thinking, it also values thinking differently about the way we view mathematics and do mathematics with our students.

Mathematics is more than just a set a rules and procedures. Until we reflect on our beliefs of what constitutes mathematics and how we teach mathematics, we will not be able to embrace mathematics as a way of thinking about the world. The framework provides us with an opportunity to reflect on our beliefs and change the way we view, teach, and learn mathematics. It also provides an avenue for doing things differently. Thinking about things differently and doing things differently promotes both teacher and student efficacy.

Teacher efficacy is the teacher's belief that he or she has the ability to influence student learning and achievement and student efficacy is the student's belief that he or she has the ability to learn (Bruce, 2013). There is a correlation between high teacher efficacy and student learning and achievement (Bruce et al., 2010). Teachers with high teacher efficacy implement effective instructional and assessment actions and demonstrate a growth mindset, which supports student thinking, learning, and achievement.

The *Four Roles of the Numerate Learner* framework places critical thinking at the forefront and provides entry points for all learners. Once we have made sense of the four roles and how they support thinking, we can begin to create an environment that embraces and elicits thinking. Providing an environment that embraces a growth mindset and values the notion that all students can make sense of mathematics is critical as we implement instructional and assessment actions that place students' learning and thinking at the centre.

Take a moment to further consider the importance of a growth mindset. Specifically, reflect on how your attitudes and beliefs about mathematics influence your day-to-day practices. There are many myths associated with the teaching and learning of mathematics, including the following:

- Only some people are good at math.
- You have to have a "math background" to effectively teach mathematics.
- Students have to know their "math facts" in order to problem solve.
- Numeracy and mathematics are the same thing.

We have addressed a few of these myths throughout this book. If we value learning, perseverance, and critical thinking, and strive to instill such qualities in our students, then we need to pause and critically reflect on such beliefs that hinder learning and influence how students, parents, and educators view mathematics. For example, we would never consciously accept these myths:

- Only some people are good at reading.
- You have to have an "English background" to effectively teach English.
- Students have to know how to accurately "spell" in order to express ideas in writing.
- Literacy and English are the same thing.

"Essentially, teacher efficacy is the teacher's self-assessment of his or her ability to support student learning. Teachers with high teacher efficacy believe that they can positively impact student achievement despite a possible range of perceived challenging circumstances (such as low socio-economic status of the students or a lack of resources). Teachers with low efficacy believe that they have a limited ability to influence student learning and achievement."
Bruce et al., 2010, p.1599

The *Four Roles of the Numerate Learner* framework is intended to engage students to not only think critically about mathematics, but also to act on this knowledge to transform a situation. The framework also provides educators with an opportunity to think critically about the teaching and learning of mathematics and act on this knowledge to implement effective instructional and assessment actions to transform the way we do mathematics with our students. The framework helps to disrupt the status quo, which often deems mathematics as rules and procedures and not as the basis for thinking, communicating, and reflecting.

The various grade levels of tasks that we have provided in each chapter are intended to prompt and spark thinking about effective mathematics instruction through the lens of the *Four Roles of the Numerate Learner* framework. The sample tasks demonstrate how we can foster mathematical understanding and thinking by asking purposeful and intentional questions that target curriculum expectations and the principles of each role. These tasks also provide a new way of thinking and learning about mathematics for *the now* that support the development of twenty-first century skills and competencies, including collaboration, communication, and creative and critical thinking.

If we deepen our understanding of the framework so that we can purposefully respond to our students' needs by using effective assessment and instructional actions, then students will become critical interpreters and reflective communicators. If we value the belief that students should have a conceptual understanding of mathematical concepts, we also then have to value the notion of teachers having a conceptual understanding of sense maker, skill user, thought communicator, and critical interpreter.

An understanding of how the *Four Roles of the Numerate Learner* framework supports the development of collaboration, critical thinking, problem solving, communication, creativity, and citizenship leads to a learning environment that is responsive to students' learning needs in the moment—for *the now*!

An Opportunity for Reflection

How could you use the *Four Roles of the Numerate Learner* framework to support interdisciplinary thinking?

Appendices

Appendix A: Features and Attributes of a Rich Task

Rich Task Features The task ...	Rich Task Attributes The task ...
Supports positive attitudes *Does the task support positive attitudes toward mathematics?*	• is motivating and values dedication and perseverance, thereby supporting a growth mindset • allows for productive struggle or conflict, where mistakes are seen as part of the learning • encourages different ways of thinking, thereby developing confidence and independence • provides opportunities for collaboration where effort is valued and perseverance is fostered
Has a curricular focus *What is the mathematical learning?*	• is connected to the curriculum • enables students to develop procedural fluency and a conceptual understanding of mathematical concepts • is aligned to the big ideas of mathematics
Provides opportunities for connections *How does the task make connections?*	• is developmentally connected to mathematical concepts across grades and strands • may connect to known contexts or personal experiences of the students • allows for students to make connections between various representations strategies
Is grounded in problem solving *Does the task encourage students to reason their way to conceptual understanding?*	• provides opportunities for students to communicate their mathematical thinking • allows students to develop, select, and apply problem solving strategies • requires explanation, justification, or proof, and thinking time • allows for developing and applying reasoning, hypothesis making, and the testing of various strategies • provides students with opportunities to reflect on and demonstrate that they are monitoring their thinking to help clarify their understanding • has an element of purposeful struggle

Is multi-representational *Does the task allow for the use of multiple tools and representations?*	• allows students to select and use a variety of concrete, visual, and electronic learning/thinking tools and appropriate computational strategies to investigate mathematical ideas and to solve problems • encourages representations of students' mathematical thinking in a variety of ways • encourages the communication of students' oral, visual, or written mathematical thinking
Supports differentiation *Does the task allow for multiple entry points for students?*	• is accessible to all learners • encourages multiple approaches to its solution • offers opportunities for students to enter into the problem in ways that are familiar or comfortable to them • provides developmentally appropriate challenges for every student
Is engaging *Does the task have the potential to engage students in mathematical thinking?*	• has the potential to spark students' natural curiosity • considers the use of visuals, video, and other approaches that appeal to the intended audience • allows for student choice and voice; students must make decisions about what to do and how to do • can be solved in a reasonable amount of time • provides opportunities for students to have their thinking valued, share their thinking, inquire, build on the ideas of others, and reconstruct or confirm their thinking

Adapted from Conversation Tool for Reflection on Mathematical Tasks, *SIM, 2015*, Rich Tasks and Contexts, *Piggott*, http://nrich.maths.org/5662, Using Rich Assessment Tasks, *Quadrini, 2011, and* Mindset: The New Psychology of Success, *Dweck, 2006.*

Appendix B: Rich Tasks – Teacher and Student Actions

Rich Mathematics Tasks	
Teacher actions ...	**Student actions ...**
• support teacher inquiry	• support student inquiry
• support a growth mindset	• support a growth mindset
• activate student thinking	• make connections to past experiences, other strands, and other curricular areas
• develop student thinking	• investigate, explore, and discover
• incorporate the mathematical processes	• reason, prove, problem solve, select tools and strategies, represent, communicate, reflect, connect
• incorporate assessment *for/as/of* learning	• are part of the assessment process
• provide a risk free environment	• feel valued and safe to share ideas
• use effective questions to support student thinking	• demonstrate their thinking in different ways
• support the development of twenty-first century skills	• demonstrate creativity, innovation, collaborating, and critical thinking
• support differentiation through the use of open-ended questions	• feel engaged and participate
• select tasks that support the development of conceptual understanding	• make sense of the mathematics
• incorporate the use of thinking tools	• demonstrate their thinking by using thinking tools

Appendix C: Reflecting on Assessment and Instructional Actions

Reflecting on our beliefs and attitudes about the teaching and learning of mathematics is an important part of the teacher inquiry process. Use the chart below to examine your current practice. Your responses will likely affirm many of the instructional and assessment actions you are presently using, but you may also discover some areas where you may wish to try different approaches to better meet the needs of your students.

1 = Never   2 = Rarely   3 = Sometimes   4 = Often   5 = Consistently

Place a "✓" in the appropriate box.

	1	2	3	4	5
1. I value different solutions/strategies to mathematics tasks from my students.					
2. I teach mathematics by using rich tasks, within a three-part lesson framework, to enhance students' mathematical thinking.					
3. Students listen to others' mathematical thinking to reflect on their own thinking during instruction.					
4. I interrelate strands of mathematics so that students are able to make connections between various mathematical concepts when I teach.					
5. I focus on developing students' conceptual understanding before procedural knowledge.					
6. I have students use thinking tools to model their mathematical ideas and solutions to tasks.					
7. I prompt students by providing effective questions to elicit and explain their mathematical thinking.					
8. I share learning goals with students so they know what they will be learning and why it matters.					
9. I provide opportunities for students to make sense of the learning goals.					
11. I use success criteria to determine to what degree a learning goal has been achieved.					
12. I communicate the success criteria to students **before** they begin a task.					
13. I develop success criteria **with** students.					

	1	2	3	4	5
14. I have students self- and peer-assess their work in ways that improve their learning.					
15. I provide descriptive feedback to improve student learning.					
16. I use assessment to inform my teaching and guide next steps.					
17. I obtain assessment information about my students' learning through a variety of means (e.g., conversations, observations, products).					

Adapted from Ross & Bruce, 2007.

References

Anderson, L. W. (Ed.), Krathwohl, D. R. (Ed.), Airasian, P. W., Cruikshank, K. A., Mayer, R. E., Pintrich, P. R., Raths, J., & Wittrock, M. C. (2001) *A Taxonomy for Learning, Teaching, and Assessing: A Revision of Bloom's Taxonomy of Educational Objectives* (Complete Edition). New York: Longman.

Anstey, M., & Bull, G. (2006) *Teaching and Learning Multiliteracies – Changing Times, Changing Literacies*. Kensington Gardens, Australia: Australian Literacy Educators' Association.

Ball, D., Hill, H., & Bass, H. (2005) "Knowing Mathematics for Teaching" *American Educator,* Fall, 14–46.

Barber, M. (2005) *Moral Purpose – Unlocking Our Children's Potential.* Webcast Source: Leadership Snapshots. Ontario Ministry of Education, The Literacy and Numeracy Secretariat, Student Achievement Division.

Base, G. (2001) *The Waterhole.* New York: Penguin Group.

Black, P. J., & Wiliam, D. (1998) "Assessment and Classroom Learning" *Assessment in Education: Principles, Policy and Practice,* 5(1), 7–74.

Boaler, J. (2015) *Fluency without Fear.* Retrieved from https://www.youcubed.org/fluency-without-fear/

Booth, D. (2008) *It's Critical! Classroom Strategies for Promoting Critical and Creative Comprehension.* Markham, ON: Pembroke Publishers.

Brookhart, S. M. (2010) *How to Assess Higher Order Thinking Skills in your Classroom.* Alexandria VA: ASCD.

Bruce, C. (2014) Professional Learning: Efficacy. *Leaders in Educational Thought.* Retrieved from http://www.curriculum.org/k-12/en/videos/professional-learning-efficacy

Bruce, C., Esmonde, I., Ross, J., Gookie, L., & Beattie, R. (2010) "The Effects of Sustained Classroom-Embedded Teacher Professional Learning on Teacher Efficacy and Related Student Achievement" *Teacher and Teacher Education. 26*(8), 1598–1608.

Chapin, S., O'Connor, C., & Anderson, N. (2009) *Classroom Discussions.* Sausalito, CA: Math Solutions.

Charles, R. (2005) "Big Ideas and Understandings as the Foundations for Elementary and Middle School Mathematics" *Journal of Mathematics Education Leadership,* 7(3), 9–24.

Comber, B. (1997) "Literacy, Poverty and Schooling: Working Against Deficit Equations" *English in Australia,* 119–20, 22–34.

Costa, A. L., & Kallick, B. (2008) *Learning and Leading with Habits of Mind.* Alexandria, VA: ASCD.

Drake, S. M., & Reid, J. (2010, September) *Integrated Curriculum: Increasing Relevance while Maintaining Accountability.* What Works? Research into Practice. Research Monograph #28. Toronto, ON: Queen's Printer for Ontario.

Dweck, C. (2006). *Mindset: The New Psychology of Success.* New York: Random House Publishing.

Fairbanks, C. M., Duffy, G. G., Faircloth, B. S., He, Y., Levin, B., Rohr, J., & Stein, C. (2010) "Beyond Knowledge: Exploring Why some Teachers are more Thoughtfully Adaptive than Others" *Journal of Teacher Education, 61,* 161–171.

Fiore, M., & Lebar, M. L. (2015) "Student Thinking for the NOW!" *Principal Connections, 18*(3).

Fiore, M., Lebar, M. L., & Scott-Dunne, D. (2014) "The Four Roles of the Numerate Learner" *Principal Connections, 18*(2).

Freebody, P., & Luke A. (1999) "A Map of Possible Practices: Further Notes on the Four Resources Model" *Practically Primary, 4*(2), 5–8.

Freire, P. (1970) *Pedagogy of the Oppressed.* New York: Herder and Herder.

Freire, P. (1998) *Pedagogy of Freedom: Ethics, Democracy, and Civic Courage.* Washington, DC: Rowman & Littlefield.

Gutstein, E., & Peterson, R. (Eds.). (2006) *Rethinking Mathematics – Teaching Social Justice by the Numbers.* Wisconsin: Rethinking Schools, Ltd.

Hattie, J. (2009) *Visible Learning. A Synthesis of Over 800 Meta-Analyses Relating to Achievement.* New York: Routledge.

Hufferd-Ackles, K., Fuson, K., & Sherin, M. (2004) "Describing Levels and Components of a Math-Talk Learning Community" *Journal for Research in Mathematics, 35*(2), 81–116.

Katz, S., & Dack, L. (2013) *Intentional Interruption. Breaking Down the Barriers to Transform Professional Practice.* Thousand Oaks, CA: Corwin, A Sage Company.

Kellner, D. (2001) "New Technologies/New Literacies: Reconstructing Education for the New Millenium" *International Journal of Technology and Design Education,* II, 67–81.

Kerka, S. (1995) "Not Just a Number: Critical Numeracy for Adults" *ERIC Digest* No. 163. Retrieved from http://www.ericdigests.org/1996-2/numeracy.html

Krpan, C. (2013) *Math Expressions.* Don Mills, ON: Pearson Canada Inc.

Lewison, M., Flint, A., & Van Sluys, K. (2002) "Taking on Critical Literacy: The Journey of Newcomers and Novices" *Language Arts, 79*(5), 382–392.

Lewison, M., Leland, C., & Harste, J. (2008) *Creating Critical Classrooms – K–8 Reading and Writing with an Edge.* New York: Lawrence Erlbaum Associates – Taylor & Francis Group.

Luke, A., & Freebody, P. (1990) *The Four Resources Model.* New Literacies & Classroom Practice. Retrieved from http://www.newliteracies.com.au/what-are-new-literacies?/116/

McLaughlin, M., & DeVoogd, G. L. (2004) *Critical Literacy – Enhancing Students' Comprehension of Text.* New York: Scholastic Inc.

Mclure, L. (2014) *Developing Number Fluency – What, Why, and How.* Retrieved from http://nrich.maths.org/10624

National Council of Teachers of Mathematics. (2000) *Principles and Standards for School Mathematics*. Reston, VA: National Council of Teachers of Mathematics.

National Council of Teachers of Mathematics. (2013) *Formative Assessment*. Retrieved from http://www.nctm.org/Standards-and-Positions/Position-Statements/Formative-Assessment/

Ontario Ministry of Education (n.d.) TIPS4RM: *Mathematical Processes*. Retrieved from http://www.edugains.ca/resources/LearningMaterials/Math-Processes/MathProcessessPackage.pdf

Ontario Ministry of Education, Curriculum and Assessment Policy Branch. (2012) *Adolescent Literacy Guide – A Professional Learning Resource for Literacy, Grades 7-12*. Toronto, ON: Queen's Printer for Ontario.

Ontario Ministry of Education, Literacy and Numeracy Secretariat. (2012) *Supporting Numeracy*. Capacity Building Series. Retrieved from http://www.edu.gov.on.ca/eng/literacynumeracy/inspire/research/CBS_SupportNumeracy.pdf

Ontario Ministry of Education, Literacy and Numeracy Secretariat. (August 2009) *Critical Literacy*. Capacity Building Series. Special Edition #9. Toronto, ON: Queen's Printer for Ontario.

Ontario Ministry of Education, Literacy and Numeracy Secretariat. (2011) *Asking Effective Questions*. Capacity Building Series.

Ontario Ministry of Education, Literacy and Numeracy Secretariat. (September 2010) *Integrated Learning in the Classroom*. Capacity Building Series. Special Edition #14.

Ontario Ministry of Education. (2004) *Literacy for Learning: The Report of the Expert Panel on Literacy in Grades 4 to 6 in Ontario*. Toronto, ON: Queen's Printer for Ontario. Retrieved from http://www.edu.gov.on.ca/eng/document/reports/literacy/panel/literacy.pdf

Ontario Ministry of Education. (2005) *The Ontario Curriculum Grades 1-8: Mathematics*. Toronto, ON: Queen's Printer for Ontario. Retrieved from http://www.edu.gov.on.ca/eng/curriculum/elementary/math18curr.pdf

Ontario Ministry of Education. (2006) *A Guide to Effective Literacy Instruction, Grades 4 to 6*, Volume One – Foundations of Literacy Instruction for the Junior Learner. Toronto, ON: Queen's Printer for Ontario.

Ontario Ministry of Education. (2008) *Data Management and Probability, Grades 4 to 6 – A Guide to Effective Instruction in Mathematics, Kindergarten to Grade 6*. Toronto, ON: Queen's Printer for Ontario.

Ontario Ministry of Education. (2010) *Growing Success – Assessment, Evaluation, and Reporting in Ontario Schools*. Toronto, ON: Queen's Printer for Ontario.

Ontario Ministry of Education. (2013) *The Ontario Curriculum Grades: Social Studies Grades 1 to 6, Geography and History Grades 7 and 8*. Toronto, ON: Queen's Printer for Ontario.

Oxford Dictionaries Language Matters. (2016) Retrieved from http://www.oxforddictionaries.com/definition/english/thinking

Parsons, S. A., Dodman, S. L., & Burrowbridge, S. C. (2013) "Broadening the View of Differentiated Instruction" *Phi Delta Kappan, 95*(1), 38–42.

Parsons, S.A. (2012) "Adaptive Teaching in Literacy Instruction: Case Studies of Two Teachers" *Journal of Literacy Research, 44*, 149–170.

Peel District School Board. (2013) *Comprehensive Literacy: Moving Forward.* Retrieved from https://hillsidemsplc.files.wordpress.com/2013/11/final-september_27-comprehensive_literacy_monograph1.pdf

Piggott, J. (2011) *Rich Tasks and Contexts.* NRICH Enriching Mathematics. Retrieved from http://nrich.maths.org/5662

Quadrini,C. (2011) *Using Rich Assessment Tasks.* Ontario Association for Mathematics Education. Retrieved from http://www.oame.on.ca/main/index1.php?lang=en&code=presmessage&chapter=32

Ritchhart, R., Church, M., & Morrison, K. (2011) *Making Thinking Visible.* San Francisco, CA: Jossey-Blass.

Ross, J.A., & Bruce, C. (2007) "Professional Development Effects on Teacher Efficacy: RESULTS of a Randomized Experiment" *Journal of Educational Research, 101*(1), 50–60.

Small, M. (2009a) *Good Questions. Great Ways to Differentiate Mathematics Instruction.* New York: Teachers College Press.

Small, M. (2009b) *Big Ideas from Dr. Small, Creating a Comfort Zone for Teaching Mathematics.* Grades 4–8. Toronto, ON: Nelson Education Ltd.

Small, M. (2013) *Making Math Meaningful to Canadian Students, K–8.* Toronto: Nelson Education Ltd.

Small, M., & Lin, A. (2013) *Eyes on Math.* New York: Teachers College Press.

Small, M., & Lin, A. (2013) *More Good Questions. Great Ways to Differentiate Mathematics Instruction.* New York: Teachers College Press.

Small, M. (2014) *Uncomplicating Fractions.* New York: Teachers College Press.

Steen, L. A. (2001) *Mathematics and Democracy: The Case for Quantitative Literacy.* The National Council on Education and the Disciplines. Retrieved from http://www.maa.org/sites/default/files/pdf/QL/MathAndDemocracy.pdf

Stein, C. (2007) "Let's Talk. Promoting Mathematical Discourse in the Classroom" *Mathematics Teacher, 101*(4), 285–289.

Stoessiger, R. (2002) "An Introduction to Critical Numeracy" *The Australian Mathematics Teacher, 58*(4), 18.

Suurtamm, C., Quigley, B., & Lazarus, J. (2015) Making Space for Students to Think Mathematically. *What Works? Research into Practice.* Student Achievement Division. Research Monograph #59. Retrieved from https://www.edu.gov.on.ca/eng/literacynumeracy/inspire/research/WW_SpaceThinkMath.pdf

System Implementation and Monitoring Archive. (2015) *A Conversation Tool for Reflection on Mathematical Tasks.* Retrieved from: http://simarchive.abel.yorku.ca/?page_id=3555

Watt, J., & Colyer, J. (2014) *IQ – A Practical Guide to Inquiry-Based Learning.* Don Mills, ON: Oxford University Press.

West, L. (n.d.) *Cultivating Classroom Discourse to Reveal Student Thinking.* Retrieved from http://www.metamorphosistlc.com

Wiliam, D. (2011) *Embedded Formative Assessment.* Bloomington, IN: Solution Tree Press.

Zwiers, J., & Crawford, M. (2011) *Academic Conversations: Classroom Talk that Fosters Critical Thinking and Content Understandings.* Portland, Maine: Stenhouse Publishers.

Bibliography

Beatty, R., & Bruce, C. (2012) *From Patterns to Algebra: Lessons for Exploring Linear Relationships.* Toronto, ON: Nelson Publications.

Boaler, J. (2015) *Mathematical Mindsets: Unleashing Students' Potential Through Creative Math, Inspiring Messages and Innovative Teaching.* San Francisco, CA: Wiley, Jossey-Bass.

Humphreys, C., & Parker, R. (2015) *Making Number Talks Matter: Developing Mathematical Practices and Deepening Understanding, Grades 4-10.* Portland, ME: Stenhouse Publishers.

Leland, C., Lewison, M., & Harste, J. (2012) *Teaching Children's Literature: It's Critical!* New York: Routledge.

Lewison, M., Leland, C., & Harste, J. C. (2015) *Creating Critical Classrooms: Reading and Writing with an Edge.* New York: Routledge.

National Council of Teachers of Mathematics. (2014) *Principles to Actions: Ensuring Mathematical Success for All.* Reston, VA: NCTM.

Parrish, S. (2014) *Number Talks: Helping Children Build Mental Math and Computation Strategies.* Sausalito, CA: Math Solutions.

Ritchhart, R. (2015) *Creating Cultures of Thinking: The 8 Forces we must Master to Truly Transform our Schools.* San Francisco, CA: Wiley, Jossey-Bass.

Smith, M. S., & Stein, M. K. (2011) *5 Practices for Orchestrating Productive Mathematics Discussions.* Reston, VA: NCTM.

Vasquez, V. M. (2004) *Negotiating Critical Literacies with Young Children.* New York: Routledge.

Vasquez, V. M., & Felderman, C. B. (2012) *Technology and Critical Literacy in Early Childhood.* New York: Routledge.

Index